Tell it to the dead

Tell it to the dead: memories of a war

Donald Kirk

Nelson-Hall nh Chicago

Acknowledgment is made to the following magazines
and newspapers in which some of the material in this
book appeared in different form:

> The *Chicago Tribune* (© 1971, 1972, 1973); *The
> New Leader* (October 1, 1973, Copyright ©
> 1973, The American Labor Conference on In-
> ternational Affairs, Inc.); "Why They Call Lon
> Nol the Mayor of Phom Phen," "Who Wants to
> Be The Last GI to Die in Vietnam?," "Banging
> Holes in the Land," "How Major Buu Fights
> his War" (© by the New York Times Company,
> reprinted by permission); *True Magazine* (©
> 1972); and *Tuesday Magazine* (© 1965).

Manufactured in the United States of America

Library of Congress Cataloguing in Publication Data

Kirk, Donald, 1938
  Tell it to the dead.

  1. Vietnam Conflict, 1961-1975—Personal narrative,
American.   2. Kirk, Donald, 1938-   I. Title

DS559.5.K57   959.704'38   75-29137
0-88229-287-0

for
Susie
who lived it too

Contents

Preface

It all happened so quickly, the collapse of the American house of cards in Indochina, that we hardly had time to understand what was going on. First they left the Highlands, then they evacuated Hue and mobbed Danang—and finally they were fleeing for their lives down the coast to Vung Tau and Saigon, itself on the verge of defeat. Most of them, the South Vietnamese whom we had foolishly tried to "Vietnamize," in the arrogant, somehow neo-colonial term, would survive. Some would not. In any case, whatever they did, they would do it without the Americans. There was, among certain commentators, the sense that the American "people," that amorphous, indefinable mass, would accept the loss of the dream, if dream is the word for it, and go on to concerns closer to home. Yet too many Americans had served and suffered in Indochina to forget so easily and so soon. One inevitably fell back on frayed memories—bits of history that helped to explain if not exactly justify the present.

It was a war ago, in September of 1965, when I first went to Saigon. I still remember the hostesses on the Air Vietnam plane on which I flew in from Hong Kong. They were wearing turquoise *ao dais,* the graceful national dress that flows over white trousers almost to the ground. I was sure they were costumed for the exclusive benefit of the assorted adventurers, grifters, journalists, provocateurs, and soldiers, most of them American, who crowded the flights in and out of Saigon. For all the "color" stories about the lost charm of the Vietnamese capital, I hadn't yet gathered that *ao dais* were really the customary attire.

Beside me on the plane was an Americanized journalist from Taiwan, who had a first name something like Jimmie or Eddie and a last name like Lee or Lo. He was wearing a cord suit, had a crewcut, and chatted from time to time with a balding, rather paunchy American, who, it turned out, was a *Time-Life* correspondent.

The *Time-Life* man was an old hand. As we were winging into the sunset near the Vietnamese mainland, he pointed toward some odd islands and explained they were once French (or American, or Chinese—I can't remember which). Actually, they were the Paracels, acquired by the French in the 1880s, conquered by Japan in World War II, ceded to Nationalist China in 1946, occupied by South Vietnam in 1954 and, finally, recaptured by Communist Chinese troops in a weekend of fighting in January 1974. Like a number of other Americans on their first trip to "the war zone," as the news agencies called it, I was not very interested in geography. I was more curious about the possibility that an artillery shell would rip through the underbelly of the plane—or that a grenade or *plastique* would explode the moment we landed. It was dark as the plane swung low on final approach into Tan Son Nhut airport, but little lights, most of them white and yellow, others red and orange neon, twinkled from the capital. The first real menace to our security, as thousands of Americans came to learn, was the throng of taxi drivers waiting to charge exorbitant rates for the ride from the airport to downtown. A smiling young man from the *Time-Life* bureau was there to meet the senior correspondent. By chance, a French photographer happened to be at the airport and recognized the Chinese journalist in the cord suit. We happily accepted lifts in the back seat of an enormous French Peugot, a museum-piece kind of car whose distinguished good looks, dating from the 1930s, were a tribute to French artistic taste if not mechanical finesse.

Again I was looking for signs of war as we drove down Cong Ly, a pot-holed two-lane road, which has since been paved by glistening brown-shouldered Vietnamese coolies, earning the equivalent in fast-depreciating piastres of two or three dollars a day under the supervision of ruddy American contractors, making it on roughly $40,000 a year, courtesy of the United States government. All I really remember from the drive downtown was that it was raining when I got off at the corner of Tu Do opposite the Caravelle Hotel. Little beggar boys asked for money outside of Brodard's café, and a wizened woman hawked newspapers. Pimps offered girls with or without hotel rooms, but a friend in Hong Kong had already suggested I stay at the Royale, a block away on the corner of Nguyen Hue, the fabled street of flowers. Burdened with only one small suitcase, I walked down the little darkened alley, past the bars from which Vietnamese girls, as pretty then as they were at the end of the war, beckoned from the doorways.

It was a typical introduction to Saigon, but it is etched more clearly in my memory than most of the depressing days spent chasing politicians and diplomats and officials or searching for stories in "the field," as Americans generally referred to the rest of the country beyond the capital. Eventually you got to know the Tu Do scene so well that you could recognize almost every beggar and shopkeeper along the street. There was one little girl whom I watched for years. When she was two or three, barely able to toddle beside her slightly older brother, she offered peanuts while holding out her hand for money. By the time she was five or six she was still selling peanuts—but now she could demand payment in advance and, if the customer were drunk, quickly frisk his pockets and run. There were the newsboys, surprisingly honest in handing out change and arranging daily deliveries. There were the Indian moneychangers, operating in their little shops behind the cover of shelves full of paperback books—always eager to buy your dollars in exchange for piastres at rates agreed upon by the Chinese businessmen who masterminded the entire black market in currency.

In a sense the Saigon scene never really changed. There were little happenings. The Miramar Hotel, with its top-floor bar, a favorite of British journalists, did not open until late in the war, 1971 or '72. The Szechwan restaurant on one of the side streets began doing a highly profitable business in '69 or '70, purveying hot, spicy dishes to Chinese and Vietnamese as well as Americans and Europeans. But Tu Do, the square between the Caravelle and Continental hotels, Nguyen Hue—they all retained their carnival-like flavor throughout the war, through rocketings and offensives, coups and crackdowns. It was the complexion of the countryside, the "field," that underwent transitions as battles surged back and forth and lines of "security" shifted, sometimes rapidly, sometimes slowly. Even during such turmoil, however, journalists grew accustomed to certain verities. You fought for seats on great C-130s to go to Danang and Phu Bai, the little town where the ever graceful imperial capital of Hue had its airport, and you rushed to jump on helicopters for shorter runs to firebases and district compounds.

If you'd seen one firebase, or district compound, or major division-level base camp, to paraphrase Spiro Agnew, you'd pretty well seen them all. The dirt, the mud, the sun, the monsoon rain drove into the souls of all those who touched the war, except possibly for some of the middle-aged bureaucrats in Saigon, hired for desk jobs and rarely interested in much more than pro forma trips to the rest of the country. It was difficult to tell who was more responsible, the Americans or the Vietnamese, for the peculiar ambience of these bases—different, somehow, from that of bases in the States or Korea or Okinawa. It was as if a firebase absorbed the atmosphere of a country where small boys sold heroin and marijuana and motorcycle drivers waited on the nearest road to rip off the unwary, and everyone spoke in the strange argot of the war—a mixture of pidgin English, French, and, every now and then, Vietnamese. ("Titi," pronounced tee-tee, was a corruption of the French *petit*. "No bich," meant "no understand," and "same-same" was English, more or less.)

Part of the flavor of the war—the dullness, the drabness, the uniqueness of it—was "the press," that odd mixture of individuals who swirled in and out of Saigon and the field, always changing but always the same. There were conservatives and radicals, intellectuals and sensationalists, those who believed that "politics" was the story, those who spent days, even weeks, at a time in the field. There was the rabble that showed up every day for the military briefings, and there were the thoughtful reporters who knew how to dissect the issues—though no one read their work very carefully. Someone, some day, will probably write a very interesting book analyzing the Saigon press corps—its idiosyncrasies, its triumphs and failings, its ability or inability to interpret what happened. In my memory, however, the reporters merely merge into the milieu of generals and GIs, officials and politicians, shoeshine boys and bar girls.

In my own reporting on the war, I was constantly frustrated by the question of how to follow politics and diplomacy in Saigon—and still keep up with events and moods in the field. Finally, in the later years, I decided the field really was more important, no matter what various analysts might deduce from Saigon politics, and I began focusing on GIs more than I had when I first went to Vietnam. In this effort I am indebted to the editors of the *Chicago Tribune,* who let me cover much of the war as I saw it, and to *The New York Times Magazine, The New Leader, Tuesday,* and *True,* whose editors also gave me the chance to write more or less as I wished. It was largely because of my experience with these organizations that I have been able to put down some of my impressions of whatever it was that happened to us in Vietnam.

chapter 1:

"Kill one...
kill them all"

Danang: May, 1972

A steady drizzle was falling on the aluminum matting of
the airstrip. The tin-roofed hangars and waiting rooms were
abandoned, their paint peeling and doors swinging loose on
their hinges. Rusted barbed-wire barriers were tumbling
down and slashed. Across Route One, endless rows of dirt-
brown hootches stretched toward the gray-green of the rice
paddies. Half-emptied sandbags were strewn around some
of the hootches, deserted except for a few forlorn-looking
South Vietnamese soldiers. An occasional jeep or truck
splashed down a dirt road, veering around potholes and
upturned oil drums.

It was my last view of what the Americans had once
called "the Quang Tri combat base." I glimpsed it in the
second week of April from the back seat of an old French
Citroën, rented for the day in the central market of Hue. We
were returning from the shot and shelled remains of Dong

Ha, a district center still loosely held by looting South Vietnamese rangers ten miles above Quang Tri and fifty miles north of Hue. Passing by the old Quang Tri base, built by American marines in the first flush of U.S. combat "involvement," one couldn't help but sense the nothingness, the futility of the American GIs whom I had interviewed there nine months before.

"Few Americans or ARVNs [Army of the Republic of Vietnam] really wanted to fight except for career-conscious officers concerned only in personal advancement," said a helicopter pilot in a reminiscing letter to me dated "31 March 72," the day on which the North Vietnamese were launching their first attacks across the DMZ, or simply "the Z," for demilitarized zone. "This insane but not uncommon zeal accounted for the death and maiming of a number of my close fellow pilots," claimed the pilot, who had been smoking pot in a back room of the hangar when I met him and his crew members on a deathly hot night in August. "Mature, responsible men," said the pilot, "allowed selfish emotion to supplant cool logic."

Neither the pilot nor his crew, at the time, had seemed particularly interested in the war itself. Their primary concern, at least then, was the army's attitude toward pot. "The nature of a marijuana 'group' is to pressure people *away* from opiate involvement," said the pilot in his letter, writing much as he had talked in our conversation. "The smokers were physically and mentally more active than nonsmokers. The smokers were more stable than nonsmokers. The best pilots were 'heads.'" The pilot's own army career had phased out about the time the army was withdrawing its last troops from Quang Tri.

"Shortly before my scheduled departure from 'Nam, I was 'busted' on suspicion of smoking marijuana," wrote the pilot. "The MPs apologized profusely, saying that they both smoked, that many of their fellow MPs were hung-up on skag [heroin], and that neither of them had ever been forced into such a ridiculous arrest before. . . . The shit hit the fan when word filtered to the top brass. They threatened me with court-martial. . . . I knew they didn't have a case and refused to oblige in the farce. I was held several days past my originally scheduled departure date from Quang Tri while all the heavies conspired as to my disposition. I received an official letter of reprimand from my commanding general and was scornfully sent on my way—with sighs of relief, no doubt."

So that was how the war had ended for the Americans in "I Corps," the name by which the American command referred to the northern five provinces before it reverted to the old French term of "Military Region One." There was little serious fighting in the later phases of the American war, just aimless hassles over pot and skag. The memory of the helicopter pilot's views, strengthened by his letter, somehow compounded the hideous irony of the loss of those ugly firebases, mud-caked or baked dry depending on the season, those remote blue-green hills once invaded daily by floundering marines and soldiers, those little "villes" of pop-can-walled hootches built of ammo boxes and 105-millimeter artillery shells—actually very good building material if one could ignore the military-style block lettering and numerals.

How many GIs had died in I Corps? "Khe Sanh," "Rockpile," "Con Tien," "Gio Linh"—the names from the old headlines and datelines read like a ghoulish roll call. American military spokesmen say they've never "broken down the count by regions." In other words, they can tell you that 40,000 or 50,000, or whatever it is, Americans have been killed in Vietnam, but they don't know exactly how many where. Let's say a third or maybe even half of them died in I Corps—perhaps as many as 10,000 in Quang Tri alone when you consider the ferocity of the defense of the DMZ at the height of the "American war" in 1967 and 1968. For what did they—we—die? The question, almost theoretical and esoteric when considered at home or even in Saigon, assumes special poignancy when I recall visits to old bases and battlegrounds, desolated GI towns and villages still scarred by barbed wire and tin sheeting.

> I been going
> Downhill every (sic)
> Since I been in
> This Lost World
> But I haven't gotten
> To the Bottom yet

The writing on the walls of the latrine stall by the GI passenger lounge at Danang air base captured the mood of the final two or three years of American "involvement." I wrote down some of the verses before grabbing a ride to Saigon after a farewell visit to China Beach, a tawdry GI "in-country rest and recreation center" set in tall pine trees and sand by a beach near Danang.

> Kill one, they call you a murderer
> Kill thousands, and they'll call you a conqueror
> Kill them all, and they won't call you anything!

The lines might not have been original, but they reflected the cynicism, the bitterness of a war that American enlisted men knew better than their officers was already unwinnable. If it was not the performance of the soldiers on the ground that ordained retreat, it was the sense of the war at home—as caught in another popular latrine-wall graffiti:

> We the *UN* known
> Do the *UN* Godly
> For the *UN* Grateful

Or, as one scribbler implored his readers, "Please don't write nothing dirty below this sign, but I have 98 days to go home and I think I'm short after a long time in this place and away from the people." He concluded, "I'm a good man, believe me, nobody wants to." Did the writers of such lines already feel they were on trial for whatever they had done in the war? If they did, it was fitting that they should finally have lost the bases for which marines and soldiers had fought the hardest. By the time I got back to Quang Tri in April of 1972, the North Vietnamese had already driven the South Vietnamese from the bases immediately below the DMZ and were about to overrun Dong Ha entirely on their way south to the provincial capital. Looking back, however, I sensed less a feeling of guilt among GIs than one of deadening boredom, of daily petty suffering, of nothingness—relieved, sometimes, by terror and cruelty.

It was that way when I visited the headquarters of the Americal division on the beaches of Chu Lai in the summer of 1971, less than a year before the last American troops finally went home. Some of the GIs at Chu Lai had found a way to occupy themselves—and to alarm the command. They were planning to hold a "peace rally" on the beach in front of the USO on July 4th, and one of them proudly showed me a special letter distributed by the commanding general to all unit commanders. The letter, couched in typical military bureaucratic style, began with the notation, "Subject: Peace Rally." It had been reported to this headquarters, the letter somberly began, "that a gathering of personnel to rally for peace is being planned on 4 July at the USO Beach at Chu Lai." This command, said the letter, "requested higher authority for an opinion on whether or not this rally would constitute a demonstration within the meaning" of certain army regulations formally banning demonstrations.

"In the opinion of higher authorities," the letter intoned, "the activities planned do constitute a demonstration within the meaning of the Army Regulation and the USARV [U.S. Army Vietnam] regulation and are therefore prohibited. Accordingly those personnel who take part in this planned demonstration will be apprehended and will be punished as deemed appropriate." But the command quickly promised to placate restless GIs with more wholesome forms of holiday recreation. "This headquarters has announced a program of entertainment for division personnel on the USO Beach during the afternoon of 4 July," said the final paragraph of the letter. "The entertainment will include floor shows, music, sky-diving, etc. This entertainment is considered an important aspect of the enjoyment of this holiday by Division personnel and will be continued as planned for the benefit of those who wish to enjoy it." Just how much the GIs enjoyed the holiday is not certain, but one of them later told me there were almost as many on-duty military policemen at the USO beach as there were off-duty soldiers. Some of the would-be demonstrators arrived with appropriate placards but were quickly dispersed.

Crusading against the war, like taking drugs, was a luxury in which soldiers in rear areas had considerably more time and freedom to indulge than did the men in the field. Several days after my visit to Chu Lai, I was riding an APC—armored personnel carrier—across a string of sandy dunes speckled by small bushes and rocks nicknamed the "Gaza Strip" by Americans who had fought over the land for most of the war. The Americans had "rome-ploughed" the strip several times, exposing the bare earth with great ploughs to uncover mines and Viet Cong bunkers, but they still had failed to drive out the "enemy." A young lieutenant, adviser to a battalion of South Vietnamese regional force soldiers, described the problems—and the utter senselessness of the mission. "This morning an RF executive officer lost his leg, and so did another ARVN soldier," said the lieutenant. "We found booby traps that were put in yesterday." In the previous two months, he reported, his RF battalion had killed six Viet Cong soldiers and captured twelve. "Very seldom will they engage in an open fight," he explained.

So we were riding on APCs to avoid the mines while the South Vietnamese trod gingerly, carefully on the ground—usually precisely in the footsteps of the man in front, who tried, as much as possible, to step only on well-used, open paths. Beside me on the APC was a young sergeant from Long Island named Andrew Hritz. "We haven't seen any kids this mission," he observed, contemplatively, as our APCs trundled down a small road. "That's a sign there's VC in the area." Occasionally, at odd intervals, we passed the burned-out remnants of old homes, identifiable by a few sticks, ancient gravestones, cement foundations, perhaps a tea kettle or piece of china. "This was a prosperous area, you can tell that," said Hritz, relieved for the moment of the tension by a fleeting thought of homes and families. "See that brush there?" he interrupted our silence. "Be one in there—a booby trap. Trip wires across the opening. Or they'll put strawmat over the hole—cover it with dirt and grass—with wires across. You won't see them until you step into it. It's a sure foot blown away. Friend of mine lost his foot that way."

We watched listlessly, broiling in the sun, as some of the ARVN reluctantly pulled a stone away from a hunk of concrete in a hollow. "Could be for a mine or a weapons cache," said Hritz. "But probably it was a hiding place." The ARVN tossed away the stone, then picked up an ornate piece of brassware, a minor spoil of war. "I'm past the point of thinking any more," said Hritz, a broad-shouldered blond who once had had a football scholarship at a large midwestern university but volunteered for the army after failing to make the team. "You're just here, everybody helps everybody else to get home in one piece." Hritz sounded almost saddened as he ruminated over the times he had spent on the Strip. "Most of the guys here count their days," he said, "but I don't—makes them seem longer. This whole outfit here is gettin' short. They all want to go home."

That night, sleeping by the APCs on the beach, some of

the other soldiers talked about the war. "The army could pull out and it'd be just titi time before the place was overrun," said a sergeant named Terry Zimmerman, a Texan. "Unless the ARVN really shape up, they're just freeloading with the U.S. here, doing as little as possible." Another interjected with his own observation. "These people here figure they have their whole life fightin' this battle. Why rush it?" Zimmerman was still talking about the army. "You're not seeing anything, riding around, losing people for nothin'," he said, "because you're not getting anything." Next morning, early, we were again "sweeping the area" on another arc back across the dunes. At some point around breakfast we trundled by a barbed-wire refugee camp. Hordes of little children ran out in hopes of GI handouts. Soldiers threw down cigarettes, and boys aged six or seven picked them up and lit them. Some of the children rubbed their stomachs, and the GIs tossed out C-ration cans. Dozens of kids pounced on them at once, and a wild fight broke out over one stray can of applesauce. The GIs shrieked with laughter as a dozen boys punched and kicked each other for the can. "Git 'im, git 'im," one of them yelled, until finally a couple of old women broke up the melee.

Not all the soldiers were so anxious for peace. "The way Nixon talks, all he wants is his POWs back," said another young sergeant, our APC commander, as we roared out of the "ville," down a long dirt road toward what the soldiers called the "redball," Route One. "That's a good idea," said the sergeant, a North Dakotan named Robert Jackson, "but what did all these fifty thousand guys die for? I think there's too much politics, really. Now they can't do anything because of fucking world opinion. All they want really is an agreement. We're blowing up booby traps and watching ARVNs get their legs blown off." You sensed the bitterness, the hardness as the sun rose higher over the dunes and slowly penetrated through our fatigues. "We should all be in the rear," said a specialist fourth class named Stephen Pulles, from Minneapolis. "We're just having people killed for nothing. There's no sense staying here, with opinion the way it is. We'll never win. We should all be in the rear until we pull out. Now it's too late because of world opinion."

It was also too late for a young POW whom we picked up at a firebase by the road. Blindfolded, hands bound behind his back, he was ordered to climb to the top of the APC and return with us to the Gaza Strip, to the place where he'd been captured a couple of days before. I tried to sense what he was thinking as we bounced back along the same road. Light froth was forming at the corners of his mouth, but there was no other sign of the terror he must have felt. Our platoon leader chatted with me about life in some small Texan town, where his father edited a weekly paper. Then, after we had turned off the road and wandered into the dunes, he ordered the GIs on the APC to put on flak jackets and helmets. South Vietnamese RF troopers on the ground began to "recon by fire" (fire blindly into the bush). It was here, around here, that they had picked up the POW.

The ARVN pulled the POW off the APC, took off his blindfold, and ordered him to lead the way into the dense grass and brush beside our trail. A few seconds later we got a radio report. They'd found a Soviet-built SKS rifle, a "Kilo Sierra," it was called, after the initials KS. "Shit, is that all?" one of the GIs muttered. "They should kill that sunuva-bitch." From the APC I could still see the bruises on the POW's neck and arms, where he'd been beaten. He was now about fifty feet away. The lieutenant was telling me how mines were set. "They'll melt the explosive from a dud round and use the fuse from the blasting cap," he said. "They can put it all in a coke can and set a trip wire." We saw the ashen remnants of cooking fires near us. "Looks like a couple of VC slept here last night," said the lieutenant. In the midst of our talk we heard the dull roar of an explosion a hundred feet or so away, in the trees where the POW was looking for mines.

The report came back over the radio. "Found a cache with two M-60 machine guns," began the American adviser who had walked with the ARVN patrol into the low shrubbery. "We got a booby trap. Two wounded." Beside us on the APC was Specialist Fourth Class Ronnie Cloud, our medic, a black with a cross stuck into one pierced ear. "A Vietnamese girl put the cross in my ear," he explained laconically. He had a twisted black shoestring necklace with a wooden image of a black power salute on the end. He kept his hair long. One thing I had noticed about him. He never moved as we were driving out, just sat there motionless on top of the APC, as if he were somehow an extension of it. Now he was talking quietly to me, in response to my questions. "Some dink POW led the ARVN to the same point yesterday," he said, "and two guys lost their legs." We got another report on the radio. The ARVN were carrying out one of the wounded, but they refused to move the other. He was the POW. He had "multiple wounds" on his abdomen, the radio crackled. "I'm going to have to go in and get the VC," the lieutenant on our APC announced. "The little people don't want to get him." Now the medic was annoyed. "I patched up three mother-fuckin' dinks before," he told me, showing some sign of emotion for the first time in the day, "and they shot them. Yeah," he said, "I'll patch this one up too."

So we rumbled through the brush, pushing the branches to either side, sitting loose and high on the APC, hoping we'd get blown far and clear if we hit a mine, and we stopped about twenty feet from where the POW was lying. The medic jumped off, brushed past some ARVN and started working on his chest. "He's dead," he announced simply, after a few seconds of attempts at artificial respiration. "Tripped on his own wire." The lieutenant looked down at the bloodied body of the POW, at the gaping, garish-red shrapnel wounds in his chest. "I'd say they blew his shit away," he said in a monotone. "OK, let's get out of here, let's get back," he snapped at the GIs on the track. But before we could begin our ride to Route One, he called for a medevac chopper. "Wounds to the abdomen, urgent dustoff," he said, as the wounded ARVN lay on a poncho. Several minutes later the bird came in amid great swirls of dust. The lieutenant was trying to explain over the radio why he had only one wounded when we had originally reported two. "The little people," he said, "it was their boy, and they want to leave him." I noticed we were, in fact, in the middle of an old graveyard. A slab of concrete bore a name, Bui Ly, and a year, 1958. Behind us one of the GIs began shooting idly into the brush. The lieutenant whirled around. "Tell that dude to knock it off or I'll have his ass."

The incident had aroused the GIs from their lethargy. "Evens the score a little," said a kid named John Kakamo, who'd been a steelworker in Fort Wayne. "I don't find this place boring. There's always something happening." Finally we were moving back toward the redball, Route One, the same road we'd traveled twice before that day. None of us talked much. I kept thinking of the POW who'd been sitting in front of me on the way out and of the flecks of foam on either side of his mouth.

It had been that way for years. Between the Tet and May offensives of 1968, while the generals still prattled about "searching and destroying," the GIs grumbled about the waste of war. It was that way when I visited the marine firebase at the foot of the Rockpile, a vicious crag jutting up like an angry fist from the Cam Lo valley just below the DMZ, defying the bravado of the bravest young men who tried to scale it. The marines, by the time I got to the Rockpile in mid-1969, were pulling out. Almost daily, truck convoys rolled through the bases below the DMZ carrying marines to the third marine division headquarters at Dong

Ha. Some of them grinned and offered the "V" sign from the backs of the trucks, others shook their fists in black power salutes, but almost none evinced much confidence in the future of the region for which they had been fighting and dying for more than four years. "Charlie's gonna kick ARVN's tail," said Lance Corporal Edward Davis, slouched in a folding chair by the Rockpile. "Every time we was out in the field, I never seen ARVN out there fighting." Davis, a twenty-year-old black from Los Angeles, thought the marines should have gone all the way to Hanoi rather than fight an enemy who could retreat beyond the borders of Laos and North Vietnam.

Now it's just going to be a stalemate," said Davis. "They're gonna come to some kind of agreement, and no one will win." Davis was no longer certain, however, whether or not it mattered how the war ended. "This is their country," he said, surveying Route Nine, once a rutted dirt road, mined and often ambushed, now a paved all-weather highway, militarily "secure," at least by day. "I don't see why we should be out there fighting for them," Davis went on. "The people up here could care less who wins the war as long as they still got their buffaloes and rice." Other marines shared much the same view. "I think we should have taken all of North Vietnam," said a lance corporal from Virginia named George Siegrist, sipping on a can of beer he had opened to celebrate his imminent departure. "In this war here Charlie hits us, and then he runs back to safety across the DMZ. That's a useless war."

Useless or not, the fighting went fitfully on. Marines admitted the tempo had declined markedly since the large-scale engagements of last year and the year before, but they pointed to a long, low-lying range, known as Mutter's Ridge, a mile or so beyond the Rockpile. "They hit us with everything on our last patrol through there." said another young lance corporal, John Rice, from San Jose, California. "We lost eighteen guys killed and twenty wounded." Rice waved languidly toward a rise only a few hundred yards from the camp. "We had a couple rifle cracks there the other night," he said. "They're waitin' for us all the time." Another marine, who had been listening to our conversation, predicted, "Charlie will try to kick us before we leave," and then would mine the road and bridges. "But they'll have a hell of a hard time," he said. "We're ready for them." That kind of big talk was typical of marines throughout the war— even though many of them suffered from the same morale and drug problems, in the latter stages of the conflict, as did the army troops.

It was difficult sometimes to imagine a war really was going on as I visited the small bases below the DMZ in the period of American withdrawal. "Alpha One" was the name of the easternmost base, a wind-blown, bunkered circle of sand several hundred yards in from the sea and several miles below the mouth of the Ben Hai River, the formal boundary between the two Vietnams. From Alpha One, the sand gradually yielded to overgrown, flooded stretches of green bush, once-fertile rice paddies now shell-pocked, mined, and inhabited only by occasional patrols of North—or South— Vietnamese troops. The next base, two miles inland, on a deserted brown-dirt road leading to the Ben Hai, was "Alpha Two." From the observation tower on Alpha Two, headquarters for a South Vietnamese armored squadron, one could see the flag of North Vietnam flapping wanly in the hot afternoon breeze at the other end of the bridge, a couple of miles away, linking North and South Vietnam.

"Must be thirty by twenty feet," the senior American adviser on Alpha Two, Major Eddie Story, remarked as the red flag with the yellow star stretched on a puff of wind and then fell limp in the ensuing calm. Flag-watching was a favorite pastime for Story, a Tennessean who'd spent the previous four months on Alpha Two. "There's nothing going on around here," he said. "We have occasional reports of infiltration, sometimes ambushes, and they fire mortars at us once in a while, but no real big action." Story added that he had seen the lights of what he thought were trucks moving by night down the highway north of the bridge where the flag was flying. As he was talking, an American observation plane flew low over the DMZ, and jet fighters above it unloaded bombs just south of the river. The explosions kicked up smoke and debris from the paddies along the banks. Earlier in the day one of the spotter planes had crash-landed into the dirt of Alpha Two after its engine had died over the DMZ. Both the pilots had escaped, but the wreckage still lay in a crumpled heap beside the observation tower. "That was the most excitement we've had in months," said Story. "You can't tell, though. They could be getting ready for something once the marines have left."

The turning point of the war, as everyone who read about it in a newspaper or watched it on television knows perfectly well, was the fighting in early 1968, the period of the Tet offensive. It was hard at first to judge the significance of Tet. You could interpret it, as many reporters did at the time, as a fantastic defeat, or you could accept the view of the American commander, General William Westmoreland, the picture soldier, that it was a great victory over the enemy. As a matter of fact, it fell into neither category, since the war was so complicated by international politics and diplomacy, but it was undeniably a turning point. With Tet the Americans realized, if they were going to keep fighting at all, it was not going to be to win. At the same time, the North Vietnamese and the Viet Cong sensed the necessity, after Tet, of lying relatively low, fighting to demoralize their foes, but not sacrificing their depleted forces until the Americans had finally had to negotiate their own withdrawal. Perhaps no confrontation illustrated the paradox of the war more precisely than did the siege of Khe Sanh, the large marine combat base on Route Nine in the northern corner of South Vietnam.

When I first visited Khe Sanh, in late January of 1968,

three divisions of North Vietnamese were just beginning to lay down their epic siege. They were rocketing the base every now and then, but marines still walked above ground in daytime and patrolled beyond the perimeter. With the onset of the Tet offensive in the northern provinces on January 30, a day ahead of the opening Tet attacks farther south, the North Vietnamese sharply tightened their squeeze on Khe Sanh. They not only attacked it frequently on the ground but dug in so close to the base that marines could no longer patrol outside the barbed wire surrounding it. And they rocketed, shelled, and mortared it so often that no one moved outside his bunker except when he had to—and then at a dead run.

The fad at the time was to compare the siege of Khe Sanh to that of Dien Bien Phu nearly fourteen years before, but the marine regimental commander at Khe Sanh, Colonel David E. Lownds, said he had never read Bernard Fall's book on the French debacle. It was just as well. The two were not comparable at all. The Americans had all the airpower they could use—an asset the French had desperately needed—and with it finally (some two months later) forced the North Vietnamese to begin retreating. By the time the siege was lifted, in early April, the marines had lost nearly three hundred dead, and the bodies of thousands of North Vietnamese lay strewn on nearby hills and valleys.

And yet the marines, in the end, lost Khe Sanh. That is, three months after the easing of the siege, the marines decided to abandon the base, exposed in the middle of a longish valley dominated by hills from which gunners could fire down on them. Marine commanders, wisely enough, no doubt, had concluded they could deploy their forces more quickly and adeptly from small outposts on top of the hills—or else by sending in large task forces to accomplish specific goals. The new approach made eminent sense, not only in theory but in practice. The marines, it seemed, had finally awakened to the realities of how to fight in Vietnam. Still, when I revisited Khe Sanh on the day the marines revealed they were leaving, I could hardly find anyone below the rank of lieutenant in agreement or sympathy with top-level strategy.

"It was just a waste," said a Sergeant Richard Morgan, battalion intelligence scout from New York. "Tactically they couldn't stop the gooks from infiltrating anyway. They just went down further south." In fact, said Morgan, "this whole country's a waste. You gotta set up positions around the villages and brainwash the people, but there's nobody left to brainwash around here." Like the marines at the Rockpile more than a year later, those at Khe Sanh in 1968 were already asking why they had fought, what was the meaning of it all. "I feel like they're defeating the whole purpose of holding it in the first part of the year," said Lance Corporal William Laines, an Alabaman. "They made such a big thing, how it was the strong point blocking all the gooks coming through Laos." Laines still looked proudly on the marine stand at Khe Sanh as "something we accomplished," but he asked me, "Why didn't they blow it up earlier, before we lost all our friends and fellow marines?"

We were standing in a jumble of sandbags and upturned earth, the remains of bunkers blown apart by North Vietnamese shot and shell. Occasionally we heard the distant thud of artillery fired from across the Laotian border six miles away and jumped in a bunker until the explosion on or near the base. I told one marine the news of the pullout. He looked at the dirt for a moment, then replied in an angry burst, "Tell it to the dead."

chapter 2:

"Peace is at hand"

The American GIs were leaving, but Vietnamese were always skeptical of promises of peace. So often, for the past two generations, from the period of the first uprisings against the French colonialists, through the Japanese occupation and the "first" Indochinese war, they had been misled and deceived. Yet, when Henry Kissinger, during the peace talks in Paris in the fall of 1972, declared that peace was "at hand," it really seemed as if Vietnam were on the threshold of a new era, not just another turn in the old war. As the peace talks dragged on and American B-52s and F-111s swept over North Vietnam, including Hanoi, in December of 1972, Kissinger's promise again seemed to have been merely an empty act of diplomacy. Then, when the Vietnam peace agreement was finally signed in Paris on January 2, 1973, Kissinger was at least partially vindicated.

In the end, however, that agreement, like the one reached in Geneva in 1954, was a transparent act of deception, a gesture that saved face for the war-weary Americans but did not prevent the killing of another 60,000 Vietnamese in increasingly fierce fighting before the year was out. In the months before and after the agreement was signed, I traveled around Vietnam asking Vietnamese what they thought of it all. I had often talked with Vietnamese about their views on war and peace but was still moved by the almost desperate yearning they invariably displayed for relief from suffering. Perhaps no hamlet was more representative than My Lai, which I visited five years after the massacre—and several days before the last American troops were going home under the terms of the agreement. In somewhat different ways, however, the people of Cai Lay district, in the upper delta, and the denizens of the urban sprawl of Saigon also reflected the agony of a populace long accustomed to lies and broken promises from diplomats wherever they debated their fate—in their own country or in Paris, Geneva, Washington, Moscow or Peking.

My Lai: March, 1973

"Certainly," the leathery-faced man remarked as we squatted on the road in the middle of the barren hamlet, "I'd be glad to tell you what happened. Why not?" It was slightly more than five years since the massacre, on March 18, 1968, of some one hundred Vietnamese civilians by a platoon of American troops, but the aged farmer recalled it all as if it had been only yesterday. "It was really a bloody thing," said the man, talking to two Americans (this reporter and David Barton, a volunteer hospital worker who had lived in the area for a couple of years and spoke Vietnamese.)

"There was blood all over these trails," he went on, pointing vaguely toward a narrow footpath leading into a clump of trees lining the famed irrigation ditch where the bodies were thrown. "The people who were wounded were coming out right here. Sometimes the people said to me later, 'You were there, why weren't you killed,' but I was out tending my cattle. Anybody who left their bunkers during the shooting was killed."

So that was how it had happened at My Lai. This, the fifth anniversary, had more meaning than most others. By now, the Americans, the soldiers that is, had finally left Vietnam, and the people of the hamlet might ponder what it had all meant, the constant apprehension punctuated by occasional moments of terror. But that morning, five years ago, oddly enough no one had been particularly afraid, the man insisted. "Nobody was around that day," he explained. "The soldiers of the National Liberation Front had already left—had gone to another place. That's why the people weren't afraid."

True, the Americans had been firing artillery rounds in the general vicinity since about six in the morning, but they were always doing things like that, that was nothing unusual. "The other side wouldn't fight here because the fields were all in the open," the man pointed out with simple logic. "When the people saw the American troops entering the hamlet, they thought there was no more danger and came from their bunkers and were shot." The old man spoke in low tones, sometimes rolling a cigarette, glad to pass the time on a warm spring day.

"We know there's supposed to be a cease fire," he was saying, "but we're still afraid of the Americans—afraid of more artillery, more bombing. I have to think that people who kill like that are very cruel. There isn't any other way to think. So many people were killed. Six in my own family—a son and daughter-in-law and four grandchildren." It was now around ten in the morning, and the narrow black-topped road stretching around the Batangan Peninsula, through the middle of My Lai and the village of Song My to Route One, was busy. Children were scampering after their water buffalo, women were carrying kindling wood and produce from the fields, and South Vietnamese soldiers were wandering by every now and then, some on motor scooters or trucks or jeeps, others on foot. Another man, much younger than the farmer, interrupted him. "The Americans came to help the government fight the Communists," he said, but the old man wasn't satisfied with such a stock explanation.

"If they came to fight the Communists, then why did they kill all the people like that?" he asked. The younger man had no ready answer. "To tell the truth," he replied, "I don't know. The Americans came to help, but they killed. I don't understand. There should have been a commander responsible for them, to keep them from sending people into a village like that." Barton remarked that there had indeed been an official investigation of the entire incident and that one lieutenant in the end had been convicted but still for some reason could stay in his home or quarters and drink beer and play cards. The younger man shook his head. "It was a whole company that fought here," he said. Something in Barton's remark about an official investigation was especially distasteful to the older one. "There've been a lot of people who have come here and asked a lot of questions," he said, "but we don't see the results. There's been more war."

Even now, the old man pointed out, no one could live in the hamlet, no one could rebuild the devastated homes. Government troops often fired from the road or from a small outpost on a hill overlooking the entire area. The younger man expanded on the theme. "You know," he said, "there were two massacres that day." The second one somehow never got publicity. Barton recalled that American military investigators had acknowledged the other one but never bothered to arrest or prosecute anyone. A hundred more people were killed in the second massacre down the road, said the younger man. "I hid in a bunker," he explained, "while my wife and some others went down the road that way. The others, those who went the wrong way, were killed." An edge of wonder crept into the man's voice as he tried to convey the enormity of the event. "They didn't kill just people," he said, as if the killing of people mistaken for enemy troops might by itself have been understandable. "They killed animals and children—everything."

"I don't know what to say, what to think," said the older one. "I just have to live. I come to tend my cattle. There's been a lot of war. We have to accept it." Some soldiers drove up in a truck and stopped beside us. At first I thought they had come to order Barton and me to leave, to return to the provincial capital of Quang Ngai some five miles to the west, but they were just idly curious. "Aren't you afraid of being captured by the Front?" asked one of them, grinning. "The Communists kill people," he said. "They are only fifty meters away. There is no security here." The Communists lately have not fired much, but the soldier's remark indicated one of the essential ironies of My Lai—and the entire war. For all the killing and suffering, this hamlet is just as "insecure" now as it was on the day of the massacre five years ago. Nothing has changed, nothing except that My Lai in effect no longer exists. The former citizens of the hamlet, those who survived the scourge, live down the road in Song My or in a typically crowded refugee camp across the river from Quang Ngai. They return to farm the fields only in daytime, if at all.

On a slight pile of earth near the road another farmer and several boys talked about what had happened. "I left in the morning when I saw the first helicopters," said the farmer. "Otherwise I would have been killed. I lost two nephews. The soldiers shot the wounded too. How do I know why they killed? A lot of the people had come in from farther out on the Batangan Peninsula because of the fighting out there. We weren't worried." But the people should have known, the farmer went on, rambling in a low voice. "There were lots of people who had already lost people in other battles." One of the worst aspects of the massacre, he added, as if recalling a long-forgotten detail, was the stench that hung over the hamlet. "We couldn't come back for two or three days, everything smelled so bad," he recalled. "It was really hard to bury people."

My Lai today looks almost like a picture of pastoral peace. The breeze gently sways the pine trees as the boys tend their cattle in fallow fields. Only an occasional distant plane breaks the silence, a reminder of the constant fact of war. "I just see neither one side nor the other has gotten anywhere," said the farmer. "The government side, with the Americans, has really fought strong with artillery and bombing, but you never see the other side. They're here, though." The farmer described himself as a person of the country to whom the main problem was survival. "The big people may have decided on a cease fire," he said, "but for us it's all the same. All we want is to be able to eat, to work our fields, and the big people won't let us do that."

A year ago, said the farmer, he had again had to flee My Lai in the face of war. This time armored personnel carriers and planes had annihilated a new cluster of buildings occupied by the men of the National Liberation Front at the start of the offensive of spring, 1972. The rubble of the foundations and the floors of the buildings were still clearly visible on either side of the road. "We used to have sweet potato fields and lots of coconut trees," explained one of the boys sitting beside the farmer, "but when the bombs fall, they cut off the trees right at the trunk." Another boy, sitting quietly through the conversation, said that he too had been at My Lai that day five years ago. He had lain at the bottom of the ditch, shielded by the dead bodies of his mother and father and five brothers, while the soldiers were shooting.

"I've been living with friends near the market down the road," he said, "and taking care of cattle. I had to get someone else to come back with me and help bury my family." The boy was seven then, twelve now. What does he think of the American soldiers five years later? Why did they come to Vietnam? Were they really cruel people? "We can't talk to the Americans," said the boy. "They don't speak our language. They were cruel, but we don't know why they came here or why they killed. All I know is my family was killed, and I feel a tightness in my chest." Nor has the suffering ended for the people of My Lai. The refugee camp where most of them now live is an enclave of crowded, steaming tents pitched behind barbed-wire barricades guarded by South Vietnamese policemen. Although these people are by no means prisoners, in the technical sense, they often cannot enter or leave without the permission of the guards, and they cannot go out at night at all. More saddening, however, they do not have enough to eat.

"It's too far to go to the fields," said a gnarled old man sitting in one of the tents. "And we have only half a kilo of rice per person per day." The men and women, passing most of their days in the dark shadows of their tents, have little better to do than to sit and talk—and remember. "It seems like just a couple of days ago, but it was really five years," said one man, reminded of the anniversary of the massacre. "Yes, I was there," he went on, somewhat contemplatively. "I was only beaten, but I lost some relatives. Then we went to the new place, but we had to run away a couple of times a year during the fighting, and finally we came here. It's been a year since we could work our fields." A woman interrupted. "We've had to run without enough to eat." Another young man spoke up: "We don't have any chance to work. The government doesn't let us go back when we wish. If we want to go some place near here, we don't need permission, but we need permission to go and work the fields." An old woman: "We really want to go back now, but they're not letting us. They say there's no security. So we stay in this one tent— sixty-four or sixty-five of us in each of the tents."

During our talk another man, a graying, tough-featured farmer, sat down and began berating us for posing so many questions. "Many reporters have come to ask us about the situation," he said, "but we have seen no results.

You come and ask people how many were killed that day. If you want to ask such questions, that is all right, that is your business, but we need help. Many reporters have come and written about us, but they haven't helped a bit. You make us very angry. We feel a tightness in our chests." There was nothing more to say. The farmer was right. We were outsiders intruding on their suffering, asking the same familiar questions but offering nothing in return for the replies. The tragedy of My Lai was not just the death of one hundred or so Vietnamese civilians. It was the loss of an entire hamlet—and a legacy of bitterness and hatred and hopelessness. It was the tragedy of Vietnam.

Cai Lay: November, 1972

They were the "Tu Kiet," the "Four Brave"—four who died fighting a foreign enemy, who gave their lives for their family, their village, and their country rather than flinch before certain execution. Even their names, typically Vietnamese, reflect their nationalism—Duc, Duong, Thanh, and Long. Beheaded by the French in 1885, they live in the "hearts and minds" of the people of this upper delta district some sixty miles southwest of Saigon. The leading officials and businessmen of the district, as well as peasants in remote villages and hamlets, contribute annually to the Tu Kiet society, which exists to maintain a pagoda built five years ago in honor of "the Four Brave ones" of Cai Lay. Duc, Duong, Thanh, and Long—their cement gravestones lie beside each other behind the pagoda, painted with blue, yellow and red inscriptions, but villagers insist loudly their spirits never died. "Their eyes did not close after they were beheaded," explains Le Van Truong, a tailor with a small shop in the central market near the pagoda. "Therefore the people believe they are saints."

The myth of the Four Brave has gained credence lately as a result of the yearning for peace among peasants in a rural region periodically afflicted by guerrilla warfare and propagandizing. Lately, as the warring factions grope tentatively toward what may prove a stopgap ceasefire agreement, the people of Cai Lay have turned toward the spirits of the Tu Kiet for guidance on what will happen next in the faltering struggle for peace. "Every day I spend quietly in the Tu Kiet pagoda burning incense and praying for peace," says Nguyen Van Huong, who has watched over the tombs of the brave ones for twenty years and now serves as caretaker of the pagoda. "I do not know what kind of peace the Four Brave ones wanted," says Huong, a thin, quiet man who speaks softly, almost haltingly, in his home several blocks away. "They died for the independence of their country. They wanted peace for their people."

The story of the Tu Kiet seems particularly relevant today because actually they surrendered to the French rather than subject their communities to complete annihilation. French officers were holding all the people of their villages as hostages in exchange for the Four Brave. If they refused to yield, the story goes, the French would behead every one of the villagers. If the Tu Kiet gave themselves up, the villagers would go free, and only the four, as leaders of the prolonged local revolt against the colonialists, would die. For the Tu Kiet, it was more important to relieve the immediate suffering of their people than to fight on for a lost cause. The symbolism of their surrender is implicit in the words of the aged caretaker as he talks of Vietnam's continuing, endless agony.

"The people here just want peace, no more killing, no more hostility," says Huong. "We should live neighbor-to-neighbor, brother-to-brother." Every day the doors of the Tu Kiet pagoda are open for mothers, fathers, sisters, and brothers offering prayers for relatives killed in the war or still fighting for one side or another. "The people are praying for peace much more now than before," Huong reports. "They come all day long, even the high district officials." Once the members of the Tu Kiet society organized a ceremony in which they prayed for peace and threw two old bronze coins to determine the will of "the Four Brave ones." If both the coins landed on the same side, it meant there would be peace. "The Tu Kiet answered our prayers," says Huong. "The coins fell the same way. There will be peace soon." Sitting beside Huong, one of his relatives nods her head and talks excitedly. "The Tu Kiet have reappeared through other people," she claims. "They say the war lasts too long and is too hard. They tell the people to prepare for peace."

But what kind of peace? Neither Huong nor the woman seems to know. "It is up to the politicians in Saigon," Huong murmurs. Among rural peasants the "modalities" of a peace formula drafted by American presidential adviser Kissinger in talks with North Vietnam's Le Duc Tho seem as unreal and academic as an exercise in calculus or nuclear physics. In the countryside, in contrast to urban Saigon, one inevitably gets the impression that the populace wants only peace without qualifications, and does not care particularly which formula the negotiators finally agree to adopt. "I always pray for an end to fighting because the civilians are caught in the middle," says a woman in a small hamlet several miles south of here. "Sometimes I listen to speeches on my radio," adds the woman, who has one son in the South Vietnamese army, "but it all goes in one ear and out the other. All I want is for my son to return home."

In the next hamlet, a man named Nguyen Van Hai recalls a series of battles along the road last May and June. "All the families had to leave," says Hai, who lives with his wife and eight of their nine children in a one-room home dominated by a small Buddhist shrine. "All the people here want is a cease-fire and peace. If it happens here with the control of the international observers, then it should make no difference if the Communists occupy the area. My family will stay on no matter because we have lived here for generations.   As a poor citizen," says Hai, whose eldest son serves in the army, "I know nothing about high politics." He gleans enough news from Saigon Radio, however, to know that "the big politicians are working for peace," and he hopes it will happen soon, "before the Communists attack here again."

Even if the war ends, the memory lingers on for Hai in the form of bits of shrapnel from artillery shells that exploded in his small rice paddy. "The pieces cut into my feet sometimes," says Hai, wincing instinctively. The pervasive influence of the war on the hamlet, typical of hundreds like it in the Mekong River Delta region, emerges in the structure of a tiny food shop one hundred meters from Hai's home. "Ammunition for cannon with explosive projectiles," say the block letters on the wooden slats, one used for crates of 105-millimeter artillery shells. Despite an external appearance of disinterest in the form of a peace settlement, the owner of the shop displays a sense of tradition that explains much about the villagers' tolerance for unending suffering. "In ancient China," he says, while proffering Coca-Cola and a sticky, locally made candy, "two warlords fought for a decade. One won because he had the full support of the people. The other lost because the people hated him." The shopowner runs through the whole elaborate tale of the warlords, but he seems quite ambiguous on the crucial point of which warlord symbolized which side in Vietnam. Such ambiguity typifies the outlook of the peasants, who never know who really is fighting—or spying—for whom.

Although the road itself is secure by day, there always are rumors of propagandizing and flag-raising by Viet Cong agents in nearby hamlets. And not infrequently the National Liberation Front resorts to terrorism, even in broad daylight, against those who somehow seem too dangerous or too closely allied to the government hierarchy in the district headquarters.

It was that way in the hamlet of My Kiem, just a mile or so from the district center. "We came here two years ago because our village was unsafe," says a young woman named Thai Thi Huynh. "My husband slept here at night but went to the old village to work in the day. He was in charge of death and birth certificates." Several mornings ago, two young men knocked on her door and asked for him. "He was not in the house but next door with his brother and a friend," says the woman. "They had not been together for a long time and were celebrating by drinking wine and eating cake." The two men in uniform, both carrying Chinese-made AK-47 rifles, walked into the house next door and sprayed fire around the room. Mrs. Huynh's husband and brother were both killed. So was Mrs. Huynh's fifteen-month-old baby, who happened to be playing there at the time.

"They tried to kill me too, but I ran away," she says. "They were agents from our old village. I do not know why they wanted to get my husband." We are talking in the same room in which Mrs. Huynh's husband died. An old woman points to the bullet holes in the furniture. Another woman picks up a piece of wood that splintered from an ancient chest. Among the tall shade trees hanging over the thatched homes, villagers gather silently, impassively, hoping to overhear the conversation. Yellow and red-striped South Vietnamese flags are painted on the doors or roofs of almost all the houses—proof that the Saigon regime controls the village in case both sides finally agree to a cease-fire-in-place. Mrs. Huynh, however, does not think in such terms as "government control" or "Vietcong control" or even "cease-fire-in-place." All she wants, she says, is a cease-fire with no more killing.

"Then I can return to my old village and farm my land," she goes on. "I listen to the radio and know that a cease-fire will happen soon. I want a cease-fire to bring independence for the country and peace for the people. It is too late for my husband, but I want a cease-fire that will let everyone do his job with no more killing, no more shooting. I want a cease-fire under any circumstances, with no more hostility." Some of the villagers smile slightly and nod in agreement. "We are afraid the VC will come back because of the killings," says a gold-toothed man sitting in front of one of the houses. "Peace depends on those in high positions in Saigon, the politicians and intellectuals," he adds, smiling sardonically. "We are only the poor people, we can do nothing."

Saigon: November, 1972

It is 6 p.m. on the ninth anniversary of the overthrow of Ngo Dinh Diem, and Ha The Vinh is sitting in his coffee shop near the race track listening to the evening news. Vinh hears the voice of President Nguyen Van Thieu warning against a "country-losing surrender" to the North Vietnamese, against falling for the "cunning tricks" of the Communists, against signing any kind of cease-fire that might compromise the country's "independence" and "right of self-determination."

Vinh has operated his coffee shop at the same corner since fleeing from North Vietnam in 1954. As a refugee, he is almost certain to agree with Thieu's stubborn stand against the cease-fire formula negotiated by Dr. Henry Kissinger and North Vietnam's Le Duc Tho in Paris. "What kind of cease-fire are they talking about?" he asks while sipping a cup of thick "cafe français." "If there is any cease-fire, we must have conditions," he explains. "We cannot accept a leopardskin cease-fire. We, the non-Communist element, would not accept it."

There are, Vinh explains, Communists who work secretly in the government. "They might hang their flags in the offices of the government and declare them Communist-held regions. That is the problem with agreeing to a cease-fire-in-place." Vinh admits his outlook may be prejudiced by his personal experience in North Vietnam, but he claims that most of his customers share the same view. In fact, it is difficult to find anyone in this war-weary capital who really welcomes the prospect of signing a cease-fire agreement of the sort proposed by Hanoi and Washington.

Thieu may not be popular, but the people of Saigon clearly share his general distrust of the terms of any agreement that permits the North Vietnamese to continue to occupy portions of the country within striking distance of the capital. The crusade against a cease-fire has assumed almost a carnival tone with the blossoming of thousands of flags on cars and taxis, outside hotels and shops, on windows and walls.

I visit a crowded alleyway near the docks on the Saigon River, expecting that here one may listen to the voices of the dispirited, the disillusioned, yearning for an end to the war—and perhaps an end to Thieu as well. In the first house I enter, one Pham Van Lieu, a graying dockworker, gladly offers his opinions. "The people suffer too much in this war, so now everybody wants peace," says Lieu. "Peace depends on the government. If it is a good government, it can make a good peace. If it is bad, it will make a bad peace. The good peace is peace which can bring reunification of the country, North and South, so people can go from place to place with freedom. A bad peace is a peace which still encourages the hatred of the two sides."

Lieu's brother, Tran Du, also a dockworker, is somewhat more explicit. "If North Vietnam accepts the plan proposed by Thieu," he says, "then peace can come—if not, peace could not come and there will be no cease-fire." Du explains that he wants a form of peace under which "anybody can do anything he likes." In other words, he says, "If I make much money, I can spend it, and nobody can control my family expenses." Du doubts if a cease-fire would really bring about this kind of peace. "This government is good because it can fight effectively against the Communists," he says simply.

In talking to the dockworkers, however, one soon

senses that the prospect of peace, or cease-fire, is hardly uppermost on their minds. For them the agreement is merely a thought sometimes mentioned on radio broadcasts. As long as the North Vietnamese and Viet Cong are not actually attacking Saigon or its outskirts, they are far more worried over such matters as rising prices. "I can make only a little money now," says Pham Chi, forty-five-year-old father of eight children. "Everything is too expensive for me." Chi looks with feelings akin to nostalgia on the era of Diem, whose assassination on November 1, 1963, is still hailed as a climactic point in the revolution of a clique of Saigon generals. "During the Diem regime, everything was cheap," says Chi. "I listened to Thieu's speech on the radio about the peace settlement, but it was much too long," Chi adds. "I forgot everything"he said. "Anyway, the people have no power to work for peace. Only the government can decide. It's their business, not mine."

One reason for the indifference with which many Saigonese seem to view the negotiations is that, except for brief periods during the Tet and May, 1968, offensives and during occasional rocket attacks, the city has remained calm. To a superficial observer, Saigon seems to thrive, with crowded markets and restaurants, busy streets and shops. One is aware of the great contrast between rich and poor, between stately French colonial-style villas and squalid slums gleaming with tin roofs, but one hardly envisions Saigon as a city at war.

"The people here have not awakened to the danger confronting our country," complains Senator Vu Van Mau, a distinguished law professor who heads a slate of antigovernment Buddhists in the Senate. Paradoxically, although Mau has often opposed Thieu in the past, he too criticizes the cease-fire plan as one that would not solve the war, would give the Communists too much territory and would subvert the independence of the central government under a supergovernment election council. "The unanimous aspiration of the people of Vietnam is to want peace," says Mau, receiving me in the office in the front room of his home in the center of Saigon. "We want peace," he says, "but we must study the modalities very carefully. If we do not, then the cease-fire will raise many more problems than it will solve.

"How can you conceive of a cease-fire-in-place?" asks Mau. "You will just have countless problems, so the cease-fire cannot be won, realistically speaking. If you display flags to show territory, you cannot show flags in the jungle and the mountains. So how can you have a cease-fire?"

The elite of Saigon, whether for or against the government, complain openly of American "sellout" and "betrayal." They reiterate the criticism of President Thieu that Dr. Kissinger should not sign a treaty on behalf of Saigon, and they claim that Kissinger does not understand Vietnam. Kissinger is "a learned man, no doubt," says Senator Nguyen Van Huyen, the Senate president. "He has traveled widely and seen many people." Senator Huyen smiles somewhat ironically. "It is another matter, however, whether he knows what is right for Vietnam."

The sense of disillusionment with the United States relates in part to the extent to which the disillusioned are dependent on American largesse for money and position. Thousands of Saigonese, if they do not actually work for Americans, realize their shops and restaurants would soon close or lose much of their business if the United States withdrew entirely as the result of a cease-fire plan. It has already happened along Tu Do, the main boulevard running from the old French-built cathedral through the center of the city to the Saigon River. Empty bars, crammed with "waitresses" ready to ply their customers with drink and good cheer, reflect the departure of fun-seeking GIs and money-laden contractors.

"Business is no good for months," says a bar girl named Phuong. "First the GIs go home and then the police close us. When we open again as restaurants, no good. Still, no customers." At the desk of a luxury hotel down the street, a clerk asks me if I think the United States will really make a deal with Hanoi. "Nobody likes," he assures me. "Everybody is afraid." Outside the door of the hotel a host of taxi drivers wait for the chance to charge exorbitant fees. "I am for President Thieu," says one of them. "No like Dr. Kissinger"—which he pronounced "Keesger."

Those who are really rich (the bankers and realtors and big store owners) are all making plans to hoard their money in foreign banks and get out of the country. Every day, says a customs officer, the well-to-do of the city send out crates full of paintings, lacquerware, heirlooms, and the like to New York, London, Paris, Switzerland—the gathering places for Vietnam's emigré population. "One thing's for sure," remarks a jaded American official. "If there really is a cease-fire, all of these people will be ready to leave the country at a moment's notice in case the North Vietnamese have the chance to attack the city."

But attack on Saigon itself at this point seems unlikely. While the rest of the country may suffer, with or without the signing of an agreement, Saigonese fantasize themselves as above the war, thanks to military defenses as well as diplomatic guarantees. It is because the capital is relatively secure, even in the midst of war, that many Saigonese fear an arrangement that might jeopardize the position of the government and provide the Communists with the chance to assume power by coup d'etat.

At the same time, the yearning for peace also seems genuine among those who have suffered personally. "I know nothing about politics," says a woman who has lost two sons in battle. "Only President Thieu knows about that. I want only peace, that is all. I want a cease-fire, but I do not know what would happen later." Beside her sits her son-in-law, an air force sergeant. "Everybody wants peace," he says, "but the Communists should not be allowed to keep territory in which to regroup their forces for later attacks. I agree with President Thieu's viewpoint."

chapter 3:

"We're here to win"

Both Vietnamese and Americans were doubtless misled by the promises of real peace at the conclusion of an agreement in Paris, but there was no greater deception than the repeated pledges of victory at the outset of direct American involvement in the war in 1965. And perhaps no single group of Americans was more grossly deceived than the black GIs, to whom military service initially provided an opportunity, a hope for escape from slights and slurs encountered in civilian life. My first assignment in Vietnam, in September of 1965, was to interview black GIs for a magazine article, a project that enabled me to visit major American bases soon after their first occupants had arrived.

Soldiers of the Big Red One (First Infantry Division) were still living in tents by the highway between Saigon and Bien Hoa when I saw them that month. An American general, addressing troops at a performance of *Hello Dolly* starring Mary Martin, told them they could expect to read of great triumphs against "Charlie" as the result of an operation he was launching in the nearby hills. (From my own subsequent perusal of *Stars and Stripes,* I gathered that his men spent most of the next few weeks flailing around in the jungle and returned with very little to show for the operation, typical of scores to follow.)

Black GIs often spoke of their own special racial problems, but their war was not that much different from the white man's. In their early exhilaration, the black soldiers exuded a sentiment shared by many if not most members of the American military machine in Vietnam. Similarly, in the closing phase of the war, the blacks, in the depths of their depression and demoralization, did not differ radically from white GIs. Thus the story of the evolution of black attitudes—the contrast between those at the beginning and end of the American involvement—really illustrates a total shift in national mood and outlook. Yet, in many of its details, the black story *was* different, particularly as racial tensions erupted in the later stages.

Danang: October, 1965

A sea breeze blew a blast of hot air and sand across the wide white wastes that stretch inland for half a mile from the South China Sea just below Danang. First Lieutenant Tommy D. Gregory, twenty-six, bit on a grain of sand, spat it out, and smiled. "Well, now, I wouldn't say these were ideal living conditions," said Lieutenant Gregory as he looked across the tent encampment of the third marine division's third tank battalion. "But I didn't join the corps to lead an easy life. That's not why I came to Vietnam either. We're here to win."

Lieutenant Gregory, a coal miner's son from Birmingham, Alabama, began dreaming of a career in "the corps" when he was a twelve-year-old student in an all-black school. "The history of the marine corps was what impressed me," said Gregory, the battalion's liaison officer. "It's a real distinctive organization and I wanted to become a part of it."

For Lieutenant Gregory, like most of the blacks with the American forces in Vietnam, the civil rights problem, Dr. Martin Luther King, and Watts are names in occasional headlines in *Stars and Stripes.* Even in the lower enlisted grades, blacks in Vietnam have discovered that the armed forces offer a degree of equality they might not expect in civilian life. Private first class John Smith, twenty-one, of Philadelphia was trudging through thick jungle in war Zone D, a Viet Cong stronghold northwest of Saigon, when I talked to him. "This jungle is their home," Smith remarked softly as he pulled a stubborn piece of vine from around his grenade launcher. "The only jungle I know is that asphalt jungle." A lanky six-footer, Smith grinned and walked on. "But I don't mind it here, not much anyway," he said. "I'm thinking of staying in the army. There's things about it I don't like, but it's all right." Smith's sentiments were echoed by many blacks to whom I spoke in four weeks of interviews throughout South Vietnam. While they did not usually articulate racial factors, it seems clear that many have found opportunities in the service that elude them at home.

"Frankly, I never encountered that much prejudice even to talk about," said Sergeant Willie G. Waters, thirty-three, of Greenville, Texas, a helicopter crew chief based in Saigon. "My platoon has Puerto Ricans, Mexicans, blacks, and whites. You just can't make any difference and run a platoon successfully." Blacks suspect discrimination in isolated cases, but virtually all agree the armed forces have gone far in eliminating the problem. "There really ain't no way of telling if a man's acting out of prejudice," said Air Force Sergeant Jimmie Robinson, twenty-eight, of Gadsden, Alabama, a crew chief assigned to F-104 jet fighters at Danang. "People come from different places and act differently. But they always have to follow orders, so it don't make much difference in the end."

To career men like Lieutenant Gregory, in fact, the racial issue seems strangely remote and academic. "I think it's a matter of difference that'll be worked out in time," said Gregory. "I never encountered any trouble myself. I always figure, if I want something, I'll get it. And I will, too." Lieutenant Gregory never doubted, for instance, his ability to get a commission. He enlisted in the corps after graduating from Alabama Agricultural and Mechanical College in Huntsville in 1961, made private first class in boot camp, and four months later entered Officer Candidates' School at Quantico, Virginia. He was graduated in the top twenty percent of his class and received a regular commission.

As liaison officer for his battalion, Lieutenant Gregory coordinates relations with regimental headquarters, South Vietnam government forces, and other marine units. He spends most of his time behind a makeshift desk in a tent but occasionally goes out on patrols and quite often visits other headquarters. "There's been a lot of cases of marines shooting other marines around here," said Gregory. "I run around finding out what other units are doing." He added with a wry smile that he was proud to say that no marines in his battalion had accidentally shot at, or been shot at by, other marines. Like Lieutenant Gregory, Army Captain Lewis W. Wright believes deeply in America's mission in Vietnam. Captain Wright, thirty-one, with the 145th aviation battalion at Ton Son Nhut, flies a UH-1B helicopter, one of the workhorses of the jungle war. He recalled an occasion in June in which his unit flew some 200 ARVN (Army of the Republic of Vietnam) troops to Dong Xoai, fifty miles northeast of Saigon. "It turned into one of the hottest battles we had gone into," he said. "The next day I had a chance to go to the battleground and see the destruction—women, children, and babies lying dead on the ground. The thing that really struck me was the senselessness of it all. I think I saw more dead women and children than soldiers."

Captain Wright said the Viet Cong had attacked an ARVN post and had lined up the soldiers and their families and massacred them all. "My answer to those who sympathize with the Viet Cong," he said, "is that if they were able to see for themselves, as I did at Dong Xoai, there wouldn't be any question in their minds as to who is cruel and who isn't. I think people who accuse the United States of wrongdoing in this war are really being unfair."

Captain Wright does not view the conflict "in terms of winning or losing." He believes the American build-up in Vietnam "has contributed a lot to stopping the fighting." The "ideal solution," he said, "would be if the people of South Vietnam would be allowed to determine the kind of government they want without threat of force or outside pressure." In his opinion, the American military push has raised "the morale of the South Vietnam forces" and infused "a new spirit in the people."

The number of black officers in South Vietnam is relatively small, probably no more than two percent of the total. Blacks who want commissions, however, have discovered they will probably be judged more fairly and objectively by military reviewing boards than by most civilian corporation officials in the United States. "Just pass the right tests and say the right things," said Navy Lieutenant Jon A. Shelton, twenty-six, who was graduated from the Naval Academy at Annapolis in 1961 and is now with the U.S. Naval Advisory Group in Cantho, a sleepy delta town fifty miles southwest of Saigon. "I don't think you'd find a better opportunity for the black than in the army," said Captain William Cummins, Jr., with the fifth special forces at Bien Hoa, twenty miles north of Saigon.

Lieutenant Shelton mans a desk in an old French yacht club overlooking the docks of South Vietnam's River

Assault Group. He lives with several other officers in a French-built house across the road and claims Cantho is "one of the nicest towns in Vietnam." Shelton, third of five sons of a Washington, D.C., Pullman car inspector, spent two years on an attack transport ship before going to Vietnam in May as assistant Fourth Naval Zone adviser. He is proud of the South Vietnamese with whom he works. "They're the best in the Vietnam navy," he said. "They're better educated, they have high morale, almost no desertions. Basically, we're winning in the delta." The final outcome, he said, will depend on "who can stay here the longest. If you sit around and wait, they're going to take it all."

For Captain Cummins, who got a regular commission as a "distinguished military student" at Morgan State College, Baltimore, his present assignment is "the greatest I've ever had." Captain Cummins has completed special forces training, cold weather mountain school, the pathfinders' course, and airborne training. "The ultimate aim for a career officer," he said, "is to be in combat. Here's where the war is going on, here's where you're needed the most. That's why I'm here."

Gripes are more common among enlisted men than officers, but not always for racial reasons. "I volunteered for the peacetime army," said one private first class, manning a radio on a patrol. "This is war, man. I want to go home." The armed forces no longer calculate the numbers of their men according to race, but informed sources estimate that blacks compose some twenty percent of the enlisted ranks in Vietnam. Their numbers are especially high in airborne outfits like the 101st division and the 173rd brigade, where some battalions are as much as thirty-five percent black. Like the white troops, blacks accept their fates in Vietnam with varying degrees of eagerness, apathy, or dislike. Discrimination, however, is a rare complaint.

Corporal Henry Whaley, twenty-five, of New Haven, Connecticut, was leaning against the turret of a marine corps tank when I encountered him. The tank was on a bluff near Danang, and he was looking through a pair of field glasses toward a village. "You see those people over there," he said. "It looks like they're running." Corporal Whaley and a second lieutenant on the tank surmised that they were Viet Cong returning from ambush points. But they weren't carrying weapons. "Can't shoot 'em unless we're sure," said the white lieutenant with a Tennessee drawl.

Corporal Whaley looked through the field glasses again and spotted some other marines herding Viet Cong "suspects" through the village. "It's not bad here," he said, putting down the glasses. "I sure wish I was home, though." He watched a crowd of peasant women follow their "suspect" husbands and sons out of the village. The sounds of the women wailing for their loved ones carried across the rice paddies. "I guess you have to do it this way," he said. "Otherwise, you'll be doing it in the United States, but it'll be rougher then."

Sergeant Robert Jenkins, twenty-seven, expressed somewhat deeper convictions, the result of twelve years of marine corps service. Jenkins, who lied about his age and joined the corps at fifteen, believes "they should take all the demonstrators at home and bring them over here." Better yet, he added, "they should let them fight for the V.C." He is convinced "those kids are just afraid to join up and fight" and that the best cure for them would be a dose of action.

Sergeant Jenkins, in charge of administration for his company, thinks the United States and South Vietnam forces have finally taken the initiative. "In August I didn't think either side was winning," he said, looking over the sandy stretches of wasteland near Danang toward the bristly little mountains where the Viet Cong are known to hide. "We first had orders not to shoot until they shot at us. Later we were told to go out and get them like we're supposed to. So now we're gonna get them."

The life of a marine in Vietnam is probably the toughest of all the American troops in the country. They sweat under the scalding sun, flounder in muddy foxholes, are constantly on patrols in search of Viet Cong. "Every marine knew what he was in for," said Sergeant Jenkins. "If they didn't want this kind of life, they could have joined the air force. It's pretty tough, but then think how the Vietnamese live. They have it even tougher." As for discrimination, Jenkins said he never really encountered it, "at least in any way that counted much."

The envy of the troops in the field are the airmen and sailors, who at least are assured of relatively comfortable bunks at night and three square meals a day. "But it isn't that easy," said Staff Sergeant Otis Boler, Jr., a jet aircraft mechanic at Danang. "You're always worried about your plane. You check over and over again to make sure nothing goes wrong." Boler, a thirty-year-old Philadelphian, had just finished "preflighting" a B-57 bomber when I spoke to him. "I can think of places I'd rather be," he said. "But I have to be here so I make the best of it."

Boler had dreamed of becoming a pilot when he decided on joining the air force thirteen years ago. "First of all, I didn't have the education," he said, "so I became a mechanic. It's the next best thing. Eventually I hope to become a crew chief." The roar of jets sweeping up and down the runways behind him occasionally made conversation impossible. "You get a chance to take a test just like everybody else," he yelled above the sound. "A lot of us that are fairly intelligent just don't have the get-up-and-go. But I've seen several black pilots, and I think there'll be more of them."

There's no question in the mind of Air Force Staff Sergeant Johnson Rooks as to which service is basically the toughest. "The air force has better people," said Rooks, whose wife and two daughters are in Savannah. "The army will take people the air force won't look at." Rooks, aged thirty-one, is a loadmaster on a C-123, an all-purpose cargo plane that lumbers through the skies above South Vietnam with the dependability of a Mack truck.

"I've flown all over Southeast Asia," said Rooks. "I've been to Bangkok—I love that place—and to Singapore and the Philippines. They work the hell out of us. Like yesterday I worked sixteen and a half hours. We were carrying chickens, ducks, pigs, ammunition, rice, passengers, everything. It's the only plane over here that can carry a decent payload—10,000 pounds—and still get into a short strip. My plane's been shot at five times. Yesterday they hit the air force letters. You don't generally feel it as such. You hear a big crack and then you know your plane's been hit. But it's hard to knock one of 'em down. It's a pretty swell plane."

Sergeant Rooks is just as proud of the pilots as he is of the C-123s. "I think we've got the best over here. I've got even more confidence in them than the plane." As for the Viet Cong, he thinks, "We've got them whipped only they don't have sense enough to know it. The Viet Cong efforts are fruitless and stupid. All they're doing now is dying and not gaining anything." While many black servicemen involved in the Vietnam conflict agree with Sergeant Rooks, some have quite a different outlook on the wisdom of America's involvement. The dissenters may be in a minority, but their views are significant, especially when contrasted with those of other servicemen in Vietnam and Americans at home.

An air force sergeant, for instance, said that two months in Vietnam were enough to give him "a very bitter attitude toward the whole conflict." The sergeant, who asked that his name not be used, said the United States "shouldn't even be here." He explained that he thought many Vietnamese citizens were simply "making money out of us" and did not really care who won the war. "I've seen so much cheating going on," said the sergeant, "it's just amazing." The sergeant denied discrimination in the air force but said, "For some blacks, with all those civil rights problems at home, it's hard to understand why we should be fighting here." At the same time, he criticized American students for "going about their protest the wrong way" and "not knowing much about the war."

An army private whom I saw unloading goods from a truck at Bien Hoa expressed somewhat the same view. "I don't know why I should be working here," he said, "when we've got enough to keep us busy in the States." He repeated the common criticism that America was involved in a situation that's "none of its business" and that the South Vietnam government was "so weak it doesn't deserve to run this country." The private, who also asked that his name not be used, admitted his point of view was not exactly popular in the barracks. "They've been listening to too much propaganda," he said. "I think some of those students are right when they say we should pull out and let the Vietnamese settle their own problems."

The armed forces have encountered some serious cases of dissidence, but it is difficult to say whether or not racial questions were involved. Three soldiers, all blacks, in the first cavalry division got sentences ranging from two to ten years for attempting a hunger strike and refusing to go with their units to South Vietnam. Another soldier, Johnnie L. Jackson of Washington, D.C., was sentenced to six months for disobeying a sergeant in the U.S. and got three years for joining the others in the hunger strike and refusing to get off the ship.

I happened to see Jackson and the three others just before their general courts-martial in An Khe, present home of the first cavalry division. "I don't think we should be in Vietnam at all," said Private Jackson. "You see these handcuffs," he said, pointing to his wrists. "That's how the army treats you." A military police sergeant—a black, incidentally—ordered Jackson to shut up. Jackson shouted to me, "You can use my name. Go ahead and use my name." And then, just to make certain, he yelled out, slowly, "That's J-A-C-K-S-O-N!" The sergeant cursed and asked me to leave. "I can't do nothin' about him," he said, "but you can help by not leading him on."

Both North Vietnam and the South Vietnam Liberation Front have tried to capitalize on America's civil rights struggle in broadcasts aimed at persuading black troops not to fight. After one of the court-martials, the Vietnam News Agency in Hanoi put out a story that concluded, "The new repressive acts further testified to the increasing fear of the U.S. imperialists in the face of mounting antiwar movement among the U.S. troops." Radio Hanoi, Radio Peking, and the Viet Cong's Liberation Radio, operated by the Viet Cong from different locations in South Vietnam, regularly report and comment on civil rights problems in America.

Yet common cause unites blacks with white troops in Vietnam more closely than at military installations in the United States. One white air force sergeant told me he believed the average black worked harder than the average white airman in Vietnam. "They want to prove they can do the job," he said. The most diehard of white southerners cooperate with blacks on duty with only occasional complaints. Some of them say blacks are "lazy," but most don't really notice if a black or white troop is assigned a particular job. Black officers are almost universally respected, and the sergeants appear as well-liked on the average as the white noncoms.

The armed forces' authority to give orders accounts for the degree of integration achieved in the years since President Truman's famous decision to break up black units. But social segregation still exists. In the mess halls, in the barracks, even in tents in the field, black tends to associate with black and white with white. There are innumerable exceptions, but the rule remains. Blacks explain they don't feel at ease with whites, and a white said, "It just seems to work out that way." At the airmen's open mess at Tan Son Nhut, white airmen almost always congregate on one side of the room and blacks on the other.

The situation is even more acute in Saigon, where hundreds of soldiers and airmen flock nightly to bars, restaurants, shops, and movies. Almost every bar along Tu Do Street in downtown Saigon is for white persons only. Blacks who wander in are greeted with curious, often hostile, stares. They complain that sometimes they are not even served. And usually the girls will not talk to them, much less go out later.

Across the Saigon River, near the docks, a row of brightly lit night clubs cater especially to blacks. It's there that black troops gather, talk to the girls, get drunk, and have their good times, at least in Saigon. Fights have broken out, but few of a racial nature. Blacks say they feel at home with their friends in the bars near the docks. "I just like to have a couple of beers and relax," said a sergeant in slacks and sport shirt. "I don't want to feel that I'm not welcome."

The bar-girls say the blacks generally treat them well and are big spenders when they have the money. The bars are slightly more tawdry than those on Tu Do, and the girls are not quite so good-looking. The blacks blame the white troops for social segregation in Saigon and in other new soldier towns such as Danang, Nha Trang, Hue, and Vung Tau. "I'll tell you exactly what happens," said a black airman in the Playboy bar, once the scene of a Viet Cong bomb blast, now dimly lit and subdued behind crossed-iron screens. "The white guys tell the girls, 'if you drink with colored guys, we won't bring you any business.' The girls don't care who they drink with but they want the business so they do as they're told."

There is another side to the story. The Vietnamese,

along with other Asians, are deeply color-conscious. They have developed a carefully graded scale, placing people with dark skins at the bottom. "They think anyone with a very dark complexion is ugly," said an American who has spent a number of years in the country and speaks fluent Vietnamese. "Some of them wouldn't drink with blacks even if the white Americans didn't care at all."

Whatever the reasons, social segregation exists in military towns in Vietnam just as in Germany, Japan, Korea, and other places where large numbers of American troops are based. So far, the issue has given Radio Hanoi and Liberation Radio little to crow about, but they did report one fight involving black and white marines in Danang. American senior officers are clearly nervous and reluctant to discuss the situation. "After all, there's not much we can do," said a lieutenant colonel in the army. "We can tell soldiers what to do on duty, but we can't order the bar owners around." The problem is not yet serious. Many troops—black and white—who do not get to Saigon are not even aware of it. The potential for unpleasantness has developed, however, and military leaders claim they are powerless to combat it.

While black troops sometimes are upset and hurt by social discrimination, they try not to let it affect their work. I spoke to several in the Casanova, a bar on the same block as the Playboy. As usual, they talked in enthusiastic terms of the American military effort. "The people at home don't know what's going on here," was the general gist of their remarks. "We're putting all we can into it" and "Listen, we're working as hard as anybody" were other observations.

But when we got to the subject of social discrimination, their attitudes changed at once. "Don't see why this has to go on. . . . It's stupid if you ask me. . . . We're in the fight the same as everyone else," they said. And they are. "I volunteered to come here," said Sergeant Willie Waters. "The main reason was, I'd never been in combat. I wanted to make sure I was capable of leading men under those conditions. This was the only war we had." Sergeant Waters, who flies in a helicopter almost every day, thinks he knows more about the war in Vietnam than about the civil rights issue. "For the 190 years we've had an army, we've never lost," he said emphatically. "The American soldier is the easiest soldier in the world to teach. It won't take us forever and a day to learn how to fight this war. We're going to win it in the end."

Saigon: July, 1971

Turn left off one of the main streets leading to the gates of sprawling Tan Son Nhut air base and you find where it's at in Saigon. It happens on "Soul Alley," where the brothers get together, get close, real tight and rap, let it all out, and none of the rabbits or lifers, as career military men are inevitably known, dares bother them. Check it out, dig it, around five or six o'clock of an evening when they start getting back from their jobs as clerks and communications specialists, security guards and drivers, or whatever else the army makes a man do in this country. The brothers, almost all of them enlisted men in olive drab fatigues, stroll down the alley while soul music blares from the little bars and clubs, and some of them settle down for a game of cards in the few hours before night falls. Then, around midnight, Soul Alley empties as they retreat to their rooms in the cement block apartment houses and homes with tin roofs that crowd the neighborhood.

"Technically, we're not even supposed to be here," says one of the brothers, talking to an intruder in the shadows of a small shop purveying cold canned soft drinks, stolen or purchased for illegal resale from the military base exchange on Tan Son Nhut. "We're supposed to be living on the base. It's the only way we can get away from the harassment, the 'man,' the 'lifers.' Here we can live the way we want and do what we want. It's home to us." Soul Alley, in fact, is home to only a small percentage of black GIs in Vietnam—200 or 300 at most, including deserters and AWOLs, some of whom have been living along the maze of surrounding walkways for months and even years. Soul Alley attracts hundreds more blacks for a few hours, an evening, or a weekend before they return to their quarters and duties at posts surrounding Saigon. Even if the majority of the approximately 20,000 blacks in Vietnam have never visited Soul Alley, almost all of them have heard of it and view it as a symbol of their desires and needs in what many of them describe as a white man's army fighting a useless war.

"You get to live with the Vietnamese. You stay in the same houses with them," says a GI, explaining the symbolism, the sense of identification, inherent in a place like Soul Alley. "You find out the problems the Vietnamese go through to live from day to day. They're striving, the same as our people. They want to progress, same as we do. Here's President Thieu staying in his palace making money, and these people are hustling for bread. Check it out. Same as President Nixon in the White House, and the blacks gettin' nothin'. There it is."

The GI, who goes by the soul name of Brother Rap, articulates better than most of his friends the underlying attitude of thousands of blacks now serving in Vietnam. It was only a few years ago, in September, 1965, that this correspondent, asked to write an article on racial problems among GIs in Vietnam, interviewed black soldiers from all services, in all regions of the country, and discovered their attitude was almost universally enthusiastic and highly motivated. They had gripes, as do most GIs regardless of racial, ethnic, or social background, but basically they liked the army, were grateful for the opportunities it provided, approved of the war and thought we were beating "Charlie," as the Viet Cong were then known. (Now GIs refer to the VC as "gooks," "dinks," and "slopes." The term "Charlie" for Viet Cong is regarded as somewhat old-fashioned.) Indeed, I often found black GIs more vocal in defense of the war than white soldiers. "The army's tough, but it's good for us," a lanky Philadelphian told me in 1965 while on patrol in jungles north of Saigon. "We can get rank here where we can't even get jobs on the outside."

"The army treats us like dirt," Brother Rap goes on, after I tell him about my first experience, nearly six years ago, in interviewing black soldiers. "If you're white and you're in the army and you don't dig black, you can be real mean. You can put false charges against us. You can give us little details." Another GI, previously silent during my conversation with Brother Rap, interrupts. "The army's the most prejudiced place I've ever been in," he says, and then unhesitatingly gives his name: Specialist Fourth Class William Gary, a twenty-three-year-old from Chicago. "I don't mind saying who I am," Gary explains. "Anybody wants to know who I am and how I feel, they're welcome to it." Gary, like most of the blacks to whom I spoke, bitterly criticizes the army for small, seemingly petty daily offenses rather than for having sent him here in the first place.

"You can go on sick call and you're black and they give you some detail," says Gary, toying a chain of beads with a black cross around his neck. "You go see the IG [Inspector General] or chaplain, and they won't do a damn thing for you. You sit around down here minding your own business and the MPs come on lookin' for you, sayin' you're AWOL."

Whether or not such complaints are entirely justified, they are representative of the changing, angry mood among black GIs. Not all of those whom I met, in interviews from the mountainous, jungle-covered northern provinces to the flatlands around Saigon, complain about racial discrimination as such, but not one of them believes, really, in either the army or the war. They are clearly attuned to both racial and student problems in the States and aver, almost to a man, that they'd rather join their brothers in "the real war back in the world" than go on fighting in Vietnam. The attitudes of black GIs to some extent parallel those of white soldiers, who are extremely embittered by their military experience, but resentment among blacks penetrates much deeper. Whites talk of returning to more or less conventional lives—homes, families, jobs and school. Blacks tend to discuss "revolution" and "liberation" from the "system" and react swiftly, sometimes violently, to racial slights and slurs. Blacks and whites, more so than at any time since the end of formal segregation in the armed forces more than twenty years ago, tend to cluster in their own cliques and rarely talk or socialize with each other. Blacks assert their identity and independence in hair styles, dress, language, music—just as they "hang together" on Soul Alley, their own segregated neighborhood, whenever they get a chance.

"If you pulled all the blacks out of Vietnam, you'd have the biggest revolution you've ever seen in the United States," says another brother whom I meet in one of the bars off Soul Alley. "You better believe," he goes on, "when Nixon pulls us out there won't be no more United States. The blacks know demolition. The blacks know how to shoot. We're gonna use all that stuff 'back in the world'" (the term GIs inevitably use to mean "back in the States".). These words may appear exaggerated, but blacks in Vietnam have begun to organize just as their brothers have done at home. During our conversation one of them pulls out a plastic card printed on one side in red, black, and green stripes. "That's the flag of the Black Liberation Front of the armed forces," he explains, noting his own name above that of the president, Bobby Wilson, on the back.

"Bobby Wilson never talks to people," says the brother, in response to my suggestion that he arrange an interview. "He's here, though. We know him." The GIs rated the Black Liberation Front and the Black Panthers as the two most influential organizations among black GIs in Vietnam.

"Go to Troop Command, Company D, across from the Pacesetter Service Club at Long Binh," one of the GIs on Soul Alley advises me when I ask where I can learn more about these organizations. The next day I hire a taxi and drive down the crowded four-lane highway from Saigon to Long Binh, the large logistics and command center some fifteen miles northeast of Saigon. I wave at the MPs at the gate, and they wave my car into the post on the incorrect assumption that I'm a civilian employee on contract with the government. Rather than look at once for the Pacesetter Service Club, I ask the driver to stop in front of the Long Binh Jail, or "LBJ," as it's generally known. (If you're black, you get put in a big box at the LBJ," Brother Rap told me at Soul Alley. "You sit in there all day with the sun beating down. You might spend your whole time there. The LBJ is really black man's university.") As I walk toward the barred front gate of the stockade, a jeep stops and three men get out, two whites and a black. The whites are guarding the black, who's just been sentenced to three months' confinement. "What for?" I ask the black. "It would take me all day to explain," he says, then raises his fist in a black power salute and disappears through the gate with his guards.

A white sentry tells me to see the stockade commandant before asking more questions. I go to the headquarters, a neat gray frame structure with clipped green grass in front, and see three blacks painting the walls. "We're parolees," explains one of them, Sergeant Charles Trigg, twenty-four, of Racine, Wisconsin. "We do outside jobs while serving our sentence." Trigg has no particular grudges against his guards inside the LBJ but talks about the circumstances of his arrest and conviction. "They gave guys promotions to say I was AWOL," he says. "My CO told me, 'If you stay in my unit, I'm gonna git you.' I was held in pretrial confinement for two and a half months. They accused me of being militant, a junkie. The first sergeant of my unit had a map of the U.S. with 'Wallace Country' written on it. That shows what kind of people they are."

Before Trigg can go on with his story, a colonel walks out the door and tells me I can't talk to parolees. He directs me to the office of the brigade public information officer, who carefully writes down a series of questions I want to ask the LBJ commandant, who later refuses to grant me an interview.

Then the brigade information officer tells me to visit the main information office at the headquarters of USARV (U.S. Army Vietnam) on a small knoll a mile or so away. At USARV headquarters a lieutenant colonel informs me of a new regulation that an information officer must escort all reporters at all times on army posts in Vietnam. He orders a young lieutenant to accompany me to the Pacesetter Service Club. I expect the lieutenant to interfere with my questions, or at least to inhibit the blacks whom I want to interview, but he politely sits a few tables away from me during private conversations.

"The colonel put me out of my unit because I was a suspected Black Panther," says the first GI whom I meet, Specialist Fourth Class Bernard Barges, twenty, of Columbus, Georgia. "The policy was to send all suspected Panthers into the field. I had a lifer looking for me. He really wanted to get me. I've been transferred eight times in nine months, and I never did anything." Another black, Specialist Fourth Class Ernest B. Stokes, twenty, of Chicago, joined Barges and me for coffee. "We had a Black Panther meeting right outside the door of the service club," says Stokes. "It was a peaceful, calm meeting. Everybody was discussing their feelings. Nothing was happening, but the MPs came down there and broke it up. If there's too many blacks in a crowd, they think we're making trouble." Barges explains that one or two men lead all black GIs in every company and try to unite them against slurs from whites. (Sergeants from rural southern or tough urban backgrounds are the ones most likely to bate the blacks.)

"They had a racial riot at the enlisted men's club a while ago," says Barges. "The whites wanted to play country western music, and we wanted soul music. Seems like every time we tried to play soul, some sergeant came along and turned it off and put on something else." The riot was not particularly serious, but it was typical of the increasing number of clashes between racial groups in the wind-down period of American involvement in the war. A few whites and blacks fought each other, crowds gathered, the MPs came, and, in this instance, the incident was over. "The next night," says Barges, "the colonel had guards lined up on either side of the street with M-16 rifles." Racial clashes of this sort occur much more frequently in rear areas, where soldiers often live in boredom with not enough to do, than on firebases and patrols in the bush, where GIs are primarily concerned with survival against always-elusive Viet Cong troops.

Like the brothers in Soul Alley, Stokes and Barges both urge me to go to Company D, Troop Command, in a row of dingy wooden barracks across the red dirt road in front of the service club, and ask some of the Black Panthers about racial incidents and provocations. "You can tell the Panthers by the black tams they're wearing on their heads," says Barges, walking me out of the service club and pointing me in the right direction. Trailed by my lieutenant escort, I enter one of the barracks and find a GI who calls himself "Brother Lacey" sitting on a bunk in his darkened cubicle. "The tam is just like a symbol of what we do," says Lacey. "A lot of guys wear peace signs on their caps, so I think we should wear black berets when we want. The CO gave five guys extra duty for wearing them." Another GI, "Brother Money," walks into the cubicle and reveals the existence of still another black organization known as PUFF, People's Union to Fight Facism.

"The pressure in this company is rough," explains

Brother Money. "We need PUFF and the Panthers to hold us together." Brother Money and Brother Lacey both agree the young whites are not particularly to blame. "The old whites are the trouble," says Money. "The only beef we got is with the old lifers, black or white. You don't have any black lifers to turn to. They think just like the old whites. They're all Toms." Money notes the black lifers refuse even to engage in the black handshake, known as the DAP, Dignity for Afro Peoples. Black GIs, wherever they meet in Vietnam, customarily exchange the handshake by banging their fists together a number of times in an elaborate ritual that infuriates most commanders and noncoms, who view it as a departure from conventional military discipline. "The Toms are afraid the man will think they want to get on with us if they go in for Dapping," says Money. "They're more white than the whites."

"They hate to see the blacks can get together," says a third GI, Sergeant Fred Wilkerson, twenty-two, of Macon, Georgia, the only one in the group who doesn't hesitate to reveal his full name. "They don't think we can get together without violence." One gesture that particularly annoyed white superiors was a daily formation called by the blacks in honor of all black GIs who've died in Vietnam. The idea, says Brother Money, "is to show the man we sympathized with all the blacks out there in the field dying for nothing." The army finally persuaded the blacks to cancel their impromptu demonstrations by sending a black civilian employee around to talk to some of them.

"He said how dangerous it could be if we continued to organize," says Brother Money. "He told me he had no sides. He didn't belong to anything. He had no right to be talking." The blacks agreed to call off some of their meetings, but their anger never faded. "This is the last war we fight," says Money. "The last generation in America sang songs and poems. The next time will be guns and rifles—at home."

Besides deepening anger and resentment among black

GIs, the war also is having another effect that frightens enlisted men and officers alike and seems to follow no racial boundaries. Blacks and whites freely admit that more than half of them have adopted the heroin habit in Vietnam and are not sure what they can do about it. "They need to get everybody out of the 'Nam because there's too much dope," says one of the blacks at Company D. "Eighty percent of the young people in 'Nam are on dope. They're all getting strung out on heroin." Another GI informs me that heroin is available for $2.50 a vial from Vietnamese outside the post gate, or $50 on post. "For $20 you can get ten vials," he says. "In the States one vial costs $160. Over here it's ninety-seven percent pure. In the states it's only fifteen percent." GIs often begin their addiction by smoking marijuana cigarettes laced with heroin and then advance to snorting and skin-popping without marijuana. Almost all GIs smoke marijuana, which few regard as a serious problem. The real menace, GIs contend, is heroin, an almost unshakable habit once it really hooks you.

The blacks at Company D, however, resent the white man's complaint that black GIs are responsible for the drug problem. "They say the young blacks are the cause of drugs here," says Brother Money, "but it's the young whites and the Vietnamese who sell it to them." Money charges that noncoms often deter black GIs from entering the army's "amnesty program" for breaking the habit. "Say I go up there and go through the program," says Money. "Then I come back here and the sergeant's been tellin' everyone I've been on drugs though he's not supposed to tell anyone. . . ."

Before Money finishes his thought the door of the cubicle swings open and a major stands framed against the light in the corridor. "I'm the information officer for the support command," he informs me. "Where's your escort?" The lieutenant, who has remained outside the room, identifies himself. The major rebukes the lieutenant for not having informed him I am here and then forbids further interviews in the barracks.

"They're afraid we gonna say something," says Brother Lacey. "We don't have any privacy at all. That's how they jump on the blacks." As I'm about to leave, Money signals Lacey, and Lacey puts on a recording of "Whitey's Got a God Complex." Blacks from other cubicles appear in the hall. They begin giving each other the black handshake, temporarily blocking the major, the lieutenant, and me as we begin to walk down the hall of the barrack to the front door. "Hey, I want to talk to the reporter," say a couple of blacks, and the major says anyone who wants to talk to me can see me in his presence in the company headquarters.

Two blacks follow us to the orderly room, where I ask more questions. The presence of the major does not bother them particularly. "The blacks get treated worse than the whites," says one of them, Specialist Fourth Class Donald Brooker, twenty-two, of Philadelphia. "When I first came, I try my best to straighten up. The lifers try to make me screw up." Brooker says he never even smoked pot before arriving in Vietnam. He doesn't admit having experimented with hard drugs, but he blames service in Vietnam for having inculcated the habit in his friends. "The main reason people use drugs is not just to escape reality but to get away from the stress and strain," says the other GI, Private Anthony Austin Dumas, twenty-one, of San Francisco. "It gets so bad here, it's the only way to relieve stress."

Brooker and Dumas basically confirm impressions I've already picked up in dozens of other interviews. I wonder, though, how GIs feel just before they leave Vietnam. Could it be they're a little happier then—willing, possibly, to forgive and forget some of the suffering they've endured in their year here? I ask for permission to visit the 90th replacement battalion, the unit through which all GIs must pass on their way from duty in the southern half of Vietnam to the United States. Army headquarters grants my request, and four days later assigns the same lieutenant to escort me to the 90th. I find several hundred GIs spending their last hours in Vietnam before boarding the "Freedom Bird" for the ride to the West Coast. Not all of them are looking forward to peace on the home front after their year at war.

"We're gonna lose here," says Specialist Fifth Class Gregory Brigham, twenty-two, of Albemarle, North Carolina. "There's too much going on 'back in the world.' That's where we're fighting the big war." Almost to a man, the blacks whom I meet at the end of their tours are planning, one way or another, to support their brothers in the States. "I'm gonna throw all my medals right on the White House steps," says Specialist Fourth Class Charles Doswell, twenty-one, of Richmond, Virginia, who spent most of his year here in an artillery battery. "I got a bronze star, and I don't know what for."

Only two or three years ago most GIs, black or white, would have been glad to have had a bronze star on their records whether it was deserved or not. Now, however, medals and rank seem to have lost much of their meaning, especially for blacks, who regard them as white men's status symbols. "Medals can't help you get a job these days," says Doswell. "Nobody cares any more." Sergeant Bobby Dozier, twenty-one, of Charlotte, North Carolina, echoes Doswell's views. "It's just a political war," says Dozier. "A bunch of people are makin' money off it." Doswell and Dozier both promise, after they return to the States, to join "some kind of black organization." Not one of the blacks whom I interview has the slightest desire to reenlist in the army after his current rour.

"Don't fight a war," warns Specialist Fourth Class Mack Hart, twenty-two, of Chicago. "That way you can't lose a war. This war doesn't make any sense. Nobody knows what the hell we're over here for." The futility inherent in

Hart's remark seems to summarize the attitude of black GIs as they look back over the history of this seemingly endless struggle. As far as most blacks are concerned, the war is already over—and lost. Now they anticipate a larger, much more important struggle for themselves "back in the world."

chapter 4:
"The whole thing's pointless"

The attitudes of GIs did not turn seriously until President Johnson stopped the bombing of North Vietnam and agreed to enter into peace talks with North Vietnam and the Viet Cong's Provisional Revolutionary Government in the fall of 1968. Until then, in visits to the field, GIs spoke optimistically, if grudgingly, of what they'd accomplished in Vietnam and often seemed rather proud to have done their time. Many of them angrily criticized demonstrators back in the States, notably those who were avoiding the draft by going to college.

The change in GI attitudes in 1969 was so sudden that I wasn't aware of it until a free-lance journalist named Ewing Carruthers told me of conversations he'd been having with GIs on firebases near Saigon. Carruthers was the first to introduce me to the new meaning of the "V" sign, a symbol I had assumed still stood for "victory" until I finally noticed that GIs who obviously were not at all concerned about winning were using it. In the spring of 1969, during a series of massive demonstrations in Washington, I visited GIs outside Tay Ninh, a town northwest of Saigon not far from the Cambodian border, and watched as some of them fired machine guns and cannon at the conical form of the legendary Black Virgin Mountain, for years a favorite VC hideout. Most of the soldiers did not sympathize much with the demonstrators, but the overwhelming sentiment was that war was a waste, that "we aren't fighting it like we should," that "we should go home and let the dinks fight their own war."

GI morale from 1969 onward deteriorated rapidly, so much so that I spent a month in the northern provinces in 1971 reporting only on GI attitudes. By this time the GIs, in far more danger from hard drugs than from the enemy, by and large applauded the demonstrators. "I wish I was there with them," was a commonplace remark. The senselessness of the struggle, at this stage, was nowhere more apparent than on the dull, desolate hills west of Danang.

Danang: August, 1971

It is late afternoon on the dirt brown outcroppings and pale green brush of Charlie Ridge, and the eighteen or twenty remaining men of the first platoon and headquarters of Delta company are slowly emerging from under their poncho liners, which they have strung up for tents to protect themselves from the sweltering dry-season sun. "Who's going on that patrol?" asks Specialist Fourth Class Garrett Gentry, a lanky Californian with a shock of sandy hair. Gentry is "pig man" (M-60 machine-gunner) and he is nearing the end of twelve months in the field. He would prefer to do as little patrolling as possible.

As if to answer the question, Sergeant First Class Louis Tartaglione, first platoon's craggy, gravel-voiced leader, announces he's heard people by the stream, a bare trickle hidden by thick underbrush at the base of the spine on which

Delta has encamped for the night—and, it seems, the day as well. No one really believes there are people by the stream. Sergeant Tartaglione, a Brooklynese known as "Tag" to the troops, admits, at the age of thirty-six, that he's "too old for this war," and it's quite possible he's confused by the sound of falling limbs or the rustle of small animals. Still, since someone must go on patrol down there, two or three GIs absent-mindedly pick up M-79 grenade launchers and squeeze off a few rounds. "If anyone's there, it'll scare 'em away," one of them remarks, as eight or ten men, not including Specialist Gentry or Sergeant Tag, get their stuff together for the walk down the slope.

The shadows are lengthening as the patrol—cursing, chattering, bunching together, breaking all the rules that sergeants once taught their men—hack their way through elephant grass and bramble that snaps back and claws at faces, sleeves, arms, and legs. Some ten miles to the east, across a flatland of rice paddies and peasant hamlets, one sees the jagged cliffs of Marble Mountain, on the coast just south of the turgid base town of Danang, built for 40,000, now teeming with 400,000, most of them refugees from peasant hamlets destroyed in more than six years of war. To the southwest, beyond more rice paddies, broken by ugly brown gashes of earth occupied by South Vietnamese and American troops, lies the "Arizona Territory," a dangerous no-man's land pocked by shell holes and booby traps, fought over incessantly by soldiers of all kinds—American, South Vietnamese (regular, regional, and popular force), Viet Cong, and North Vietnamese. South of the Arizona Territory, running almost to the sea, rises a range of slate-gray peaks, once the scene of daily firefights between U.S. marines and North Vietnamese, now largely left to the latter except for intermittent air strikes and haphazard patrols.

The marines, after having campaigned up and down the northern provinces of South Vietnam since 1965, finally vanished a few months ago. Army officers now walk the graceful tree-shaded grounds on the Han River in Danang from which marine generals directed operations from the beaches of Chu Lai to seasonally muddy or dusty firebases along the DMZ. An army colonel lives in a house atop "Freedom Hill," a barren outcropping just west of Danang air base, from which a marine major general led a 22,000-man division. The colonel, Rutland Beard, a well-groomed Washingtonian in command of a brigade of 6,000, sends his forces over precisely the same country once traversed by marines—the lowlands, the Arizona Territory, Charlie Ridge to the west, and some of the mountains beyond. "We should have been out of here two years ago," says Beard, an army war college graduate who would doubtless have been relieved for expressing such heretical views in 1969. "Let some other people police up the world," he adds, during a visit to one of his firebases, a patch of dirt on a steep promontory west of Charlie Ridge. "We have enough problems in CONUS [Continental United States]. We should clear up the mess at home."

Later, over a drink in an air-conditioned officers' club, also built by the marines, Colonel Beard, who commanded a battalion to the south on his first Vietnam tour in 1966, revises his statement to conform with national policy. "I feel that I will have accomplished my mission," he says somberly, "if we can get out of here with as few casualties as possible and still accomplish the task we're assigned"—the defense of Danang and environs, including one of the three largest airbases in the country and supply, support and logistical facilities for U.S. forces spread up and down Military Region One, the five northernmost provinces. Except for occasional isolated forays, the colonel readily concedes, American troops have ceased pursuing the enemy much beyond the first few ridge lines. Among some 70,000 GIs in the entire northern region, no more than 8,000 are beating the bush at one time—and the number may be considerably less than that by the end of the year.

Yet, if there *is* any war, that is, an American war, involving American troops and costing American lives, it is mainly here in Military Region One, once known as "I Corps," whose mountains and rice paddies have absorbed more American blood than the other three regions combined. "We've lost eighteen men in our company in the month of July to booby traps," says Sergeant Tag, biting off his words in a Brooklyn accent that's safely survived seventeen years of service, including a previous tour in Vietnam. "All we get out of it was killing two dinks in an ambush." Half a dozen GIs were sitting around an old shellhole eating C-rations when one of them tripped on a hidden wire, setting off a boobytrap concealed in the hole. Three men were wounded—two of them partially blinded, one with possible brain damage. "There all night and nothing happens," says a rifleman, recounting the incident as we pause by the stream. "Sit here and watch a buddy get blown away. The whole thing's pointless. We'll never win."

It is, in reality, a desultory kind of struggle, punctuated by occasional explosions and tragedy, for the last Americans in combat in Vietnam. It is a limbo between victory and defeat, a period of lull before the North Vietnamese again seriously challenge allied control over the coastal plain, as they did for the last time in the Tet, May and September offensives of 1968. For the average "grunt," or infantryman, the war is not so much a test of strength under pressure, as it often was a few years ago, as a daily hassle to avoid patrols, avoid the enemy, avoid contact—to keep out of trouble and not be the last American killed in Vietnam.

"I mean, what does it accomplish? What does it gain?" asks the Delta company forward observer, a captain who attended officer candidates' school after having graduated from the University of Southern California in Los Angeles. "Even if we kill 500 dinks, to me it's not worth it." The FO (forward observer) calls in artillery strikes on suspected targets in the nearby hills, but he does so with notable lack of relish. "I just saw three dinks down in that rice paddy," he says. "One of them was carrying a shiny tube. They were probably VC, but maybe they were civilians with an old shell. I don't think it's right to look for some excuse for shooting at them." Although the FO is an officer, a captain, he articulates the views of the GIs with whom I go on patrol down the ridge.

"The dinks are just playin' with us, waitin' for us to go home, then they'll beat the shit out of the ARVN," says the rifleman in front of me, reiterating a view held by many of his superiors. "It's a lifers' playground, a chance for the generals to test their strategies," the GI enlarges, in thick Georgian tones, as we scramble up from the streambed, only to stop again a minute later so our pig man can test-fire his machine-gun. "Git them cows down there," another GI yells, grinning while the M-60 spews a torrent of bullets into the bushes in front of us. The cows, grazing on a rise half a mile away, amble off at the urging of a boy who hears the shots. A couple of grunts idly curse all the lifers, the CO, the NCOs, anyone vaguely responsible for issuing them orders and threats. "If the lifers don't get you," says one soldier, explaining why we don't radio a false location and rest instead of walk, "then the VC will."

Their chatter is hardly unique. In a month visiting units in the field and rear areas around Military Region One, I found literally no young GIs in favor of the war, none who didn't think we should get out, few who didn't hate the lifers almost as much as the "dinks," a term sometimes used to describe ARVN as well as enemy forces. For all the complaints, though, cases of refusals to fight or go to the field are quite rare—perhaps an average of two or three per battalion per month. Virtually every GI in the bush theoretically yearns for a softer job somewhere else, but almost all of them admit that time slips by faster here, that "lifers don't hassle you so much" over petty matters of haircut and dress, that drugs are less available and duty not so dull as in the rear.

Nor are there more than slim odds these days that a combat GI will die despite the danger of mines set and reset daily by VC sympathizers—often farmers or small boys selling PX Cokes by the road at fifty cents a can. Casualty figures in July receded to the lowest ebb in six years: eleven killed one week, twenty-nine another, approximately seventy for the month, the first since 1965 in which the number of American "KIAs" was below one hundred. (The U.S. command now emphasizes low American casualties with the same enthusiasm that it once accorded such statistics as enemy "body counts." At a briefing in the middle of August, for instance, a military spokesman proudly disclosed a weekly average of nineteen American KIAs for the previous two and a half months, "exactly half the average of thirty-eight KIAs for the year to date." These figures, he noted happily, were low compared to an average of eighty-one killed each week of last year.) Specifically ordered to hold down casualties, commanders rarely invade traditional enemy base areas among shadowy crags and valleys to the west, and they carefully disengage from battles in the lowlands if heavy losses seem inevitable or even conceivable.

"There's no longer that intense aggressiveness," laments Lieutenant Colonel Lee Roberts, who enlisted in 1948 at the age of nineteen, attended OCS after having been turned down for West Point, and now commands a battalion from a mountain firebase twenty miles southwest of Danang. "Instead of going on lengthy sweeps our companies set up defensive positions from which they send out patrols," he explains, sipping coffee from a paper cup in front of his sandbagged command bunker overlooking an undulating velvet-green valley. "If they get into contact," he says, surveying his AO (area of operations) through baleful, slate-gray eyes, "they back off and call in air and artillery."

"What we're performing is defense-in-depth," summarizes the information officer at the headquarters of the Americal division, which includes the 196th and two other brigades. "We're interdicting enemy supply routes and infiltration of troops to the lowlands." Off-duty, in the officers' club behind the headquarters, built on rolling sand dunes at Chu Lai for which marines fought bunker to bunker in 1965, a couple of ROTC lieutenants joke about the Americal's notorious past. First there was exposure of the massacres at My Lai, a few miles to the south, followed by the case of a former brigade commander charged with mowing down civilians from his helicopter and, late last year, revelation of the use of a chemical defoliant capable of inducing cancer. Then, in June, the commanding general was relieved in the aftermath of an attack on a firebase in which thirty-three GIs were killed—the worst such disaster of the war.

"I'm afraid to tell anyone back in the world I'm with the Americal," says one of the lieutenants, laughing sardonically. "No one has much pride in the division. That's one reason morale is so bad."

Despite the image, however, the mission of the Americal, and the attitude of its men, is no different from those of the only other full-strength U.S. division in Vietnam, the 101st airborne, based at Camp Eagle, midway between Danang and the DMZ. Just as the Americal defends Danang and the coast to the south, so the 101st patrols the lowlands and hills beyond the one-time imperial capital of Hue, for political and cultural reasons South Vietnam's most important city after Saigon. Once regarded as the toughest of U.S. divisions, the 101st now appears as wary of combat, as reluctant to fight, as lax in discipline as the Americal. Commanders proudly evoke its traditional nickname "Screaming Eagles," but GIs these days prefer to call it, not without a certain touch of reverse pride, "the one-oh-*worst.*"

"I have seen the Screaming Eagles in action—in the jungles and air and assisting the people of northern Military Region One—and can testify that the outstanding reputation enjoyed by the 101st is completely justified," brags the division commander, Major General Thomas M. Tarpley, somewhat defensively, perhaps, in a letter on the inside front cover of the division's slick-paper color magazine, *Rendezvous With Destiny.* The cover itself, however, testifies to the war-weariness of the men whom Tarpley tries to praise. In a water-color sketch of defoliated trees etched against glowering gray clouds, three GIs are standing on a truck, reaching toward a crane helicopter hovering above them. Black peace symbols adorn drab army-green cannisters containing 155-millimeter artillery shells, and the twisted limbs of three leafless trees form the initials FTA— Fuck the Army.

Already a legend around the 101st, the cover evokes the mood of the grunts whom I accompany on a couple of patrols by a stream along which the VC slip men and supplies into the lowlands. The platoon leader is a gung-ho career soldier, a first lieutenant out of OCS, airborne, ranger, and jungle schools, who inwardly regrets he's arrived in Vietnam a couple of years too late for "the real war." He has been here only three weeks, and he wants to play by the rules. Maybe, if he succeeds, there's still enough time for him to get a regular, as opposed to a reserve, commission, a promotion to captain and command of a company in the field, if not exactly in full-fledged combat.

"Shoot to capture, not to kill," the lieutenant (an athletic lifeguard type with close-cropped hair and finely sculpted features that remind me of a carving of a Roman centurion) earnestly abjures his troops, in an upstate New York twang. The men—saddled up for RIF (reconnaissance in force) through abandoned rice paddies and one-time hamlets, erased except for occasional cement foundations by air and artillery strikes—grin and snicker. "I shoot for KIAs not POWs," retorts Specialist Fourth Class Robert Latchaw, a wiry Pole from South River, New Jersey, laughing at the lieutenant's naivete. "Whaddya want us to do, shoot an ear off?" jibes "Doc," the medic. The lieutenant, unfazed, insists he's following policy set down by "higher higher" headquarters. "We're not after body counts any more," he says. "We'd prefer information. KIAs don't talk." With that, we sally forth through tall grass toward a stream near which our platoon sergeant, remaining behind with a squad, swears he saw "two dinks running that way."

It is clear to everyone but the lieutenant, though, that we're not seriously pursuing the dinks. "Just walking' around don't accomplish nothin'," says Latchaw, a church-going Catholic with a wife "back in the world" who sends him weekly packages of "world food," good canned stuff to supplement the boring, bland diet of C-rations. "I been here nine months, and I ain't been in no firefight yet. Most I did was spend one hundred days in the mountains during the monsoon without changing my clothes once." We are, by this time, beside the stream, filling canteens, after an hour-long stroll broken by frequent halts for rest and talk. If there are any VC in the area, they are as eager to keep out of our way as we are to keep out of theirs.

All of us, that is, except for the lieutenant: next morning, around ten, he leads another RIF toward the stream, this time aiming for the "draw," the ravine down which the water tumbles from the last ridgeline into the lowlands. Before we begin it seems like another easy walk in the sun, but our point man is still hacking away with his machete several hours later. (Murmurs from the grunts behind me: "I want to be back in Kentucky rabbit-huntin'." "When I get back to the world I don't *even* care if I see another forest. I'm stayin' in the city.") The lieutenant sends a Chicano named Quito and the Kentuckian into the bush in hopes of finding an easier route. They return a few minutes later. "Gettin' too theek," says Quito. "Might see some dinks we don't want to see." We plunge straight ahead, find a trickle of flowing water, fill canteens, keep going another hour until we stumble on the same stream we reached, lower down, on yesterday's patrol. Some of the men flop in, lying on their backs in the fast-running water, cleansing bodies, fatigues, and socks. We would be easy marks for an ambush. No one is standing guard.

Across the stream we see clear signs of VC movement— little footpaths leading across open clearings. For the first time we spread apart, a routine precaution. Behind us rises the slope of the ridgeline, burned off by a fire ignited by one of the Delta Tangos ("Defensive Target" artillery rounds) called in by the lieutenant a couple of nights ago. We follow the path along the stream, wade in the water for a while, then emerge about where we'd been the day before. A couple hundred yards from the bank a neat path cuts a straight line through the bush—the kind of trail along which guerrilla soldiers could run full-speed if necessary, dropping for cover at the sound of approaching helicopters. "We're going to work this area really well," the lieutenant advises his men, who remain sullenly silent. "We're gonna set up ambush positions in here and set out a couple of claymore mines. We'll get them as they fall back from fighting the ARVN." As soon as we return to our original position, the lieutenant announces his plan to our platoon sergeant, a hard-talking midwesterner who's been with the unit only a couple of days but knows how to handle eager young officers.

The sergeant reminds the lieutenant a resupply helicopter is about to arrive, that it'll take a while sorting out the stuff, burning off the waste. He says he's found a "beautiful NDP [night defensive position] over there by the trees." The lieutenant hesitates, wavers. He senses that his men, from the new sergeant on down, are against him. "We don't have enough men for an ambush," the sergeant argues. "We get into a fight, we'll get waxed." The lieutenant finally settles for placing a single claymore on the trail this side of the stream.

That night we hear the crackle of small arms from near the ARVN positions, a mile or so away. Helicopters circle overhead, muttering machine-gun fire, and artillery and mortar rounds thud across the fields. Next morning, the lieutenant is beside himself with anger and frustration. "Should have sent out that goddam ambush," he says, not looking at the sergeant. "Could have gotten the bad guys running away. Godammit, we gotta get moving. It's late already. This happens again, I'm gettin' everyone up at five o'clock." It is ten-thirty before the men are ready. Then the lieutenant gets more bad news, this time over the radio. The battalion commander, on a firebase a couple of miles away, is ordering the entire company in to guard the base perimeter: "just routine rotation." In vain the lieutenant pleads that he needs "a couple more days to work the area by the stream." His men curse him silently. "Godammit, if no one was looking, I'd frag the sonuvabitch," says one of them.

The threat of fragging (explosion of a fragmentation or hand grenade) in this case is probably not serious. The GI who makes it not only walked point the morning before but willingly went on patrol again in the evening to plant the mine. An Iowa farm boy, he criticizes the war on the grounds that "We're not fightin' it like we should." Since we failed to invade North Vietnam, H-bomb Hanoi and Haiphong and declare "free fire zones" of VC hamlets, he says, "we oughta quit wastin' time and go home." Like most of the grunts in the field, he may lack motivation but he's not really bored.

It is mainly in the rear, among the troops whom the grunts disdainfully call the REMFs, for Rear Echelon Mother Fuckers, that talk of fragging, of hard drugs, of racial conflict seems bitter, desperate, often dangerous. At the combat base at Quang Tri, the last provincial capital below the DMZ, I walk into a dimly lit single-story barrack one afternoon hoping to find perhaps a couple of GIs with whom I can talk—and count sixteen of them reclined in the shadows of a lounge shielded by blankets and curtains hanging from the windows. "Welcome to the head hootch," says a thin, hollow-cheeked private first class of eighteen or twenty, waving me to a spot on the couch after I convince him I'm a reporter, not a criminal investigator. The GIs proudly explain that their hootch is a meeting place for potheads from all over the base, but I don't smell any marijuana in the air. "How many of you smoke skag?" I ask. They all raise their hands.

Why have they "graduated" from pot to heroin? They are, for the most part, white, with ten to twelve years of education, a few with records of juvenile delinquency or petty crime in civilian life. While some might not perform well under any circumstances, all of them seem hopelessly demoralized both by the war and by their immediate surroundings. "I was supposed to be a heavy equipment operator but all I do is pick up beer cans," says one. "They haven't got anything for us to do," says another. "They just want to keep us busy." Several are aimless drifters, too strung out for work, awaiting courts-martial or undesirable discharges, demotions, and restrictions. Many, if they report for duty at all, put in only a few hours a day before finding some excuse to return to the hootch—or else they just go back with no excuse at all.

It's far from clear whether the men are more at odds with their commanders and sergeants or the war in general. "They tell you to do something, then they yell at you for doing it," says the equipment operator. "They harass you about haircuts and beards and burn you for sleeping on guard when you've been working all day." Most of their complaints are petty, often unjustified, but they also suffer from the same sense of futility, of pointlessness, that affects thousands of other GIs in the midst of withdrawal of American troops. "The gooks are winning this war," says one. "The ARVN are afraid to fight. They run away. The gooks can have the place when we leave."

While we are talking, one of the heads slowly stirs a plate of "hard times," all-but-powerless marijuana seeds and stems. "It's what I got left." he says. "It's gettin' so hard to score marijuana around here, guys have to turn to scag"—which doesn't smell, comes in much smaller quantities and is easier to hide. Another GI idly tells a story, verified by his friends, of ordering more than 300 vials of heroin at two dollars a vial from a Vietnamese "cowboy" on a motorcycle at the gate of the base. "I gave him $200 for a hundred and grabbed the rest and ran," says the GI. "He drove away grinning, and I knew *I* was the one that was ripped off. It was all salt and sodium acid." The next day the GI, armed with his M-16, bought 200 vials from a trusted pusher in a nearby village. "I sell it here for five dollars a vial," says the GI, a personable, fair-haired midwesterner who served six months of a five-year term "back in the world" before enlisting in the army.

That night a couple of the GIs—a black and a Chicano—invite me to a pot party at a helicopter hangar on the other side of the runway. The air in the little room in the back of the hangar is heavy with the sweet smell of "dew." A helicopter pilot tells me he's been "stoned ever since getting to Vietnam," that he performs better that way but is "scared shitless of skag." Beside him is a doctor, an army captain, silently smoking pot in a corncob pipe. Some of the helicopter crewmen pass freshly rolled cigarettes around. A couple other GIs stand lookout, glancing from time to time over the walls to see if MPs are coming. One of the chopper pilots argues convincingly for legalization of pot—says it's not habit-forming, is no more harmful than beer. He doesn't know it, but several of the enlisted men in the room have laced their marijuana with heroin. Some of them plan to go to "the party after the party"—an all-night get-together in one of the perimeter bunkers for speed freaks, pill-poppers who get them by mail from home or else buy them on the local market, often at ordinary pharmacies.

It is difficult to quantify the use of drugs in the rear. It is obvious, though, that a relatively high proportion of the

REMFs, perhaps twenty percent, are on the hard stuff, as opposed merely to marijuana, while in the bush only a marginal few indulge. ("We see a guy using it out here, we take care of him, or the CO sends him back to the rear," one of the men on Charlie Ridge tells me. "Otherwise he'll be high some time when we're under attack. You can't hardly walk if you're high all the time.") The use of drugs in base camps accounts for widespread thefts and also is a major factor in fraggings. GIs on drugs will steal almost anything, ranging from stereo sets to food from the mess hall, to sell in exchange for heroin, peddled by small boys and women, cowboys on Hondas, even South Vietnamese soldiers operating near Americans.

Addicts resort to fraggings—or threats and intimidation—whenever commanders order shakedown searches, restrict them to quarters, or otherwise attempt seriously to cut down the flow. At each camp I visit there are tales of incidents in which GIs have blown up orderly rooms, sometimes wounding or killing the wrong man, or merely exploded grenades outside windows for shock effect. One of the favorite techniques is to set off a tear-gas cannister, a harmless antic that creates momentary chaos and serves as a warning of more violence later. At the rear headquarters of one of the battalions of the 196th brigade, on a road leading to Freedom Hill outside Danang, the battalion's new executive officer, in the midst of a crusade against drugs, walks into his quarters one day and finds a grenade pin on his pillow—a symbol of what may happen to him if he keeps up his campaign.

"It's like war, you take chances," says the exec, Major John O'Brien, a bluff, outspoken man with a strong Massachusetts edge to his voice, who served ten years in the enlisted ranks before attending OCS. The major, on his second tour in Vietnam, arrived here in June totally unprepared for the new mood among GIs in the rear. He found heroin vials, empty and discarded, around battalion headquarters, in the latrines, under barracks. At least twenty of more than one hundred men assigned to his battalion "rear" were perpetually too high and too weak to perform. At the same time, numbers of others were not only opposed to the use of drugs but willing to work with him to prevent it. "We had a couple of meetings just brainstorming," says O'Brien, who, unlike many career officers, seems capable of talking with young GIs on an informal basis. "We were receptive to any ideas anyone wanted to offer. The situation was so desperate, we had to be open to everything." The result was a well-balanced combination of force and propaganda.

"As of this date I'm declaring war on drug abuse in this battalion," begins the mimeographed "Open Letter to All Drug Users," posted on bulletin boards around the battalion area. "I will seek out and find every drug user and pusher" in the battalion. The letter recounts what many of the GIs already know—that the major, assisted by a special "drug squad" of half a dozen men, has already confiscated more than one hundred vials filled with heroin. "Things are going to get a hell of a lot tighter before the problem is satisfactorily resolved," the letter promises. "There will be more shakedowns and inspections. The flow of traffic in and out of the compound is going to be dramatically reduced. My officers and senior NCOs are now authorized to conduct unannounced search of any man on this compound." The letter invites addicts to turn themselves in voluntarily to the army's amnesty program, under which they can spend several days in a special ward getting over the immediate physical effects of the habit—or else face prosecution and court-martial.

Major O'Brien has no real illusions, however, about the long-range efficacy of his program. He thinks he's drastically reduced the use of heroin in his own compound but points out a couple of cases in which addicts went through amnesty "withdrawal," only to pick up the habit again a few days later. He doesn't like to talk about the grenade pin left on his pillow (he fears that publicity might encourage a fragging) but points with a grin at a copy of his open letter, scrawled with defiant notations. "Happiness is a Vial of Smack," says one of them. "Major O'Brien is a Smack Freak," says another. "Stay a Head." Perhaps over-optimistically, the major views the comments as a good sign. "It shows they're worried," he says. "At least I'm getting a response."

Major O'Brien's program, I discover, is the exception, not the rule. By far the majority of the commanders and executive officers whom I meet are simply not aware of the scope of the problem in their own units. They tend, in many cases, to rely on the word of their NCOs—many of them so conservative, not to mention so hooked on alcohol, as to distort their whole attitude toward the drug problem. Another complication is that officers and NCOs also must cope with racial conflict in the form of protests against authority by young blacks who claim the army discriminates against them. Racial tension, like drugs, is of secondary importance in the field, but it threatens to explode in base camps where blacks have time to form their own Panther or antiwar "liberation" organizations and chafe under petty harassment by lifers who often, in fact, do reveal instinctive, subconscious, if not explicit forms of prejudice.

The racial question is so sensitive at Camp Baxter, on a road lined with military installations and Vietnamese refugee shanties near Marble Mountain, just south of Danang, that military officers don't want to let me on the base. Finally the camp commander, Colonel Joseph Otto Meerboth, a graying West Pointer, agrees to let me talk to GIs, but asks me to "come back tomorrow" when I show up for my appointment. As I am escorted toward the gate, he orders military policemen to seal off the post to intruders and search the barracks for half a dozen blacks, whom he's convinced are plotting a major racial disturbance. The next day, Colonel Meerboth explains that the blacks, transferred four days ago to another base, returned without warning to pick up their possessions and that one of them, at least, is "extremely dangerous."

"He's organized an extralegal confederacy," says the colonel, who admits having had little experience with either drug or racial problems before his assignment to Camp Baxter last fall. "The traditional method for rendering extralegal confederacies ineffective is to dismember them. Last night I brought in three of these men one by one, talked to them, and told them they had to leave. They have been escorted elsewhere." Colonel Meerboth's decision, however, has not necessarily conquered the problem, characterized by intermittent demonstrations, a couple of killings, secret meetings, and threats, spread over the past eight or ten months. At the service club, where he reluctantly permits me to interview GIs, both blacks and whites criticize the transfer of troublemakers and claim the one singled out by the colonel as the ringleader was actually instrumental in keeping the blacks from staging an armed, open revolt.

"A white man just don't understand the problem," says Sergeant Clarence Chisholm, a graduate of the Tuskegee Institute who was drafted into the army and works as a communications specialist. "Whenever you try to explain what's happening, you're branded as a militant." Chisholm, due to rotate home from Vietnam in a couple of days, charges the white officers and NCOs with practicing de facto segregation by recommending transfer mainly for blacks and leaving the camp, once twenty percent black, almost entirely white. Some of the whites whom I meet agree with Chisholm's interpretation. "Our sergeant told me, 'It's open season on blacks,'" says one of them. "The thing is this Colonel Meerboth cannot control this compound," says another, shouting excitedly in the middle of a circle of white soldiers who rush to the service club to talk to me when word gets around "there's a reporter there."

The GIs charge all the "undesirables"—Black Panthers,

drug addicts, whatever—were transferred to three or four nearby units reputed to be dumping grounds for those not wanted elsewhere. The black "ringleader," I learn, has gone to Chu Lai, where he's now on permanent guard duty with the 277th supply and service battalion. "I'm scared to go there," says another GI, a Chicano, who's also been transferred to the 277th but has returned to Camp Baxter to pick up his stuff and has somehow escaped the colonel's notice. "I hear they're *all* skag freaks down there." Intrigued, I go to Chu Lai the next day to meet the colonel's nemesis, Specialist Fourth Class Loyle Green, Jr., a tall, polite one-time student at Malcolm X University in Chicago, who once had visions of attending OCS and making a career in the army but has since decided "to help the brothers back in the world."

"They gave us five hours to pack our bags and leave after they notified us of our transfers," says Green, whom I meet in battalion headquarters. "We started to protest, but there was nothing we could do. We were railroaded to Chu Lai. The majority of the transfers were from minority groups—blacks, Spanish, Indians." Green attributes his transfer to his role in leading a sit-in in front of Colonel Meerboth's headquarters in protest against the pretrial confinement of a black GI charged with assaulting a white. "It was so tense that a lot of blacks had gotten weapons," says Green, "but it was going to be a peaceful protest." The blacks, he notes with pride, simply turned their backs, got up, and left when Colonel Meerboth emerged to order them to disperse. Then, says Green, there was a plan to destroy the entire compound, which is large enough for several thousand men. "I talked to a couple of the blacks and told them there was no way. We were already infiltrated by informants. We had the weapons and grenades to do it, but we would have lost in the end."

Green, acknowledged by Colonel Meerboth as a "persuasive speaker" and a "natural leader," appears less than militant in his outlook. Rather, he displays a sensitive judgment of power realities, an understanding of the limits to which the blacks can go, and determined, passive defiance of white authority. One factor that may have cast him as a sinister figure, in Meerboth's mind, was the funeral service in March for a black killed by a white in a brawl in the middle of the camp. "The blacks didn't want the chaplain to speak," says Green. "We had two or three hundred there. We just turned our backs to the chaplain while he kept rattling on. We chanted 'Black Power' and put up a liberation flag. It had a black fist in the middle with the words 'Black Unity' in black letters on top, with a red background. The colonel stood there shaking his head. I told him we didn't want any American flag there. No blacks are American. I don't consider myself an American. I consider myself a black."

Green, like many of the black GIs, wears the black power band, made of black shoelaces, around his wrist. A black power ring, in the form of a clenched fist, gleams from the index finger of his right hand. In defiance of authority, he is growing a full-scale beard, in addition to the regulation mustache. Ironically, in view of his antiwhite, antiwar outlook, he has never been disciplined, court-martialed, or reduced in rank. He does not refuse to go to work, as do many blacks, particularly those on drugs. "I was a clerk-typist and a driver," he says. "It was challenging at first, but there wasn't enough to do"—an explanation, combined with opposition to the war, that may account for most of the army's problems in the rear.

Unlike Green, however, most of the GIs whom I meet at the 277th headquarters in Chu Lai seem depressed, openly, dangerously rebellious, possibly on the verge of armed revolt. One of them, interviewed in the presence of the battalion executive officer, tells me the blacks have a "secret arms cache" and plan to start using it "if things don't let up around here." The exec, Major Robert De Biasio, who has been trying to work with the blacks to find the causes of their problems, listens without interrupting. Later he tells me he doesn't think the black is kidding. "We've searched those barracks time and time agan and found nothing much," he says. "I think they have the arms underground somewhere. The only way we could find them would be to order everyone out of the barracks early in the morning, keep them under guard, and go over the whole area with a mine detector."

Major De Biasio may face a tougher problem than does Major O'Brien at Freedom Hill. At the 661st ordnance company, GIs estimate that twenty percent of the more than one hundred troops don't work at all. The commander, a pleasant, open man with eight years enlisted time behind him before he went to OCS, may be afraid to impose tight discipline. He arrived several months ago, after the fragging of the quarters of his predecessor, who escaped unharmed but severely shaken. "We have some outstanding young men here," the CO blandly observes, venturing that only a dozen men in the entire battalion "use drugs on a somewhat irregular basis." In view of the CO's easy-going tolerance, it is not surprising that many of the troops whom I meet at the 661st focus their complaints on their sergeants rather than on the officers. Ironically, the most feared of the NCOs is a black, a thirty-three-year-old Georgian known for his skill as a boxer and judo expert and nicknamed, as a token of both respect and dislike, "Karate Joe."

Karate was sipping beer with another NCO, a white sergeant from Tennessee, when I interviewed him in his hootch. He's afraid to go to the enlisted men's club. He doesn't want the men thinking he's trying to harass them off duty. He's stopped counting the times he's found grenade pins on his pillow or has been threatened verbally. "It doesn't even bother me any more," he says, but it is clear he is intensely unhappy. "My first tour here, we were all together," he says. "We worked as a team. I was doing the same thing then, running the ammo supply point, humping ammo into helicopters to take to the field. I never had no problems with the men. This time they don't really care no more." Karate shouts and curses his men to work, but he's beginning to feel he's engaged in a lost cause. "You discipline them so much and eventually the CO gets started on getting them 212s"—discharges on grounds of unsuitability or unfitness for service. "I just don't know what the answer is," he says, clenching his beer can. "It's not the same army any more."

The only real answer, as far as *this* war is concerned, may be to keep withdrawing the men on an accelerated timetable and send only volunteers for the remaining advisory and rear-area jobs. Wherever I go in the northern provinces, whether in the field or in rear areas, I find the problem of motivation so overwhelming as to defy rational solutions and programs other than withdrawal. Below Charlie Ridge, on the Arizona territory, I talk with a young captain on his first tour. He is a West Point graduate, in command of a troop of armored personnel carriers—an ideal position for a career-minded military man. He has been here only a week, but already he is filled with doubts and questions.

"They train you, send you to schools," says the captain, as we begin a bumpy ride through fields planted with mines and booby traps, "but nobody's prepared to see a guy killed or wounded. I had the most sobering experience of my life yesterday—I saw one of my men wounded with shrapnel. He's the first guy I've ever seen wounded. Once we've decided to get out, and then keep fighting, it seems kind of worthless. Nobody wants to be the last guy to die in Vietnam." That night, after the APCs have formed a defensive circle by a small river, a lone guerrilla fires an AK-47 rifle from a couple hundred meters in front of us, sending bright red tracers over our position. The GIs leap onto the tracks, answering with machine-guns and M-16s. Helicopter gunships arrive, spraying the bushes with bullets. Against the black backdrop of the sky and mountains, it is an eerie late show, and it lasts for an hour.

"They got some nerve opening up against all our firepower like that," says one of the GIs as the guns fall silent and we stretch out to sleep on cots behind our track. "Far as I'm concerned, they can have this whole country. There ain't no reason for us bein' here. We was fightin' to win, that'd be one thing, but we're just wastin' time." It is a typical GI commentary, one I hear countless times around Military Region One, at the butt end of a bad war.

chapter 5:

"John Wayne would have dug it"

For a brief period in 1972 the Nixon-Kissinger policy of withdrawal from Vietnam amid "Vietnamization" and negotiations for peace appeared in serious question. The North Vietnamese and Viet Cong on April 1, 1972, opened their greatest offensive since Tet, 1968, this time sending tanks as well as infantry across both the demilitarized zone and the Cambodian border northwest of Saigon. President Nixon responded by resuming the bombing of North Vietnam, which the Air Force had already been doing in secret on a more limited scale for several months, and shelling the coastline.

American information officers, who had been eager to publicize military activities at the beginning of the war, prevented reporters from visiting the air bases in Thailand on the spurious grounds that they were technically Royal Thai property. And they claimed they did not have the aircraft to fly us to navy carriers from which planes were also flying over North Vietnam—even though such facilities had always been available in the early years of the war. They did, however, finally relent to the extent of letting us onto navy cruisers and destroyers off the coast of South Vietnam, thus enabling me to glimpse the combat from an entirely different perspective. The views of navy officers and sailors, the latter perhaps influenced by bitterness that erupted in fighting and near-mutiny at several American bases, were much the same as those of soldiers and marines on the land. There were differences, though. The days at sea produced their own kind of boredom, and the sailors could never glimpse or intimately sense the suffering of the land which they were assigned to bombard.

For all the antiwar sentiment, however, there were always the buccaneer types who would volunteer for any kind of fight anywhere—if the price were right. After the last American warplanes had ceased bombing Cambodia, in August of 1973, I met a couple of them flying a cargo plane and eager for more action. Their outlook reflected the thinking of thousands of Americans who came to Indochina on lucrative contracts. Some of them, as they lounged in luxury apartments and villas and piled up enormous bank accounts, even believed in what they were doing.

Aboard USS *Providence*: **May, 1972**

Through the binoculars on the signal bridge one discerns specks of people walking along a beach littered with sampans and hootches. Beyond the beach rise green rice paddies and woods fading rapidly into a distant skyline of blue peaks and haze. Occasionally, one also sees white or black puffs of smoke hovering on the horizon, but for the most part the view of Quang Tri, the first South Vietnamese province to fall entirely to the North Vietnamese in the current offensive, is deceptively tranquil and calm.

It is only at odd interludes, in fact, that the air force spotter plane swinging lazy circles some ten miles inland finds a target worth a shot. Then, if he does happen to see a bunker complex or supply dump or barge, he radios the nearest ship—at the moment one of three cruisers, including the *Providence,* or a dozen destroyers patrolling a 200-mile stretch of coast south from the DMZ. An officer in the combat operations center, two decks below the main deck of the *Providence,* "sights" one or more of the ship's five guns with a computer, then calls a petty officer in one of the two turrets and tells him to load.

On the bridge, Captain Kenneth G. Haynes, the skipper, a pleasant Texan whom most of the men seem to like, watches while one of the ship's six-inchers, the largest size gun on the vessel, roars and sends a 130-pound projectile over the shoreline a couple of miles away. Several minutes later Lieutenant Commander Gerald Anderson, assistant weapons officer, standing on the deck below him, shouts back the good news from the FAC (forward air controller), the term for the propeller-driven spotter plane. "Several trucks destroyed, several structures destroyed, several secondaries," says Anderson. Haynes, who has already noticed the cloud of smoke rising from the explosion, smiles approvingly.

"That's pretty good," he says, with an air of understated modesty. "You have to remember we're firing at fifty-gallon oil drums at ten miles." His smile broadens. "It would appear we've stopped effective movement of their supplies," he says. "This morning we've also been shooting at three tanks." He doesn't yet know what happened to the tanks, but later one of the enlisted men on the signal bridge offers a somewhat irreverent account of the incident. "We chased this tank right down the road," he says. "We must have fired fifty rounds and never touched it. Finally the men inside all jumped out and hid in a hootch. Then one of our rounds got them all in the hootch and tac air (fighter planes) got the tank."

The memory of the tank chase provides a moment of

sardonic humor on an otherwise dull day. Since arriving "on line" off Vietnam on April 28th, the ship's crew of more than eight hundred officers and men have been standing watch six hours on and six off, a wearisome routine that slowly tightens nerves and frays tempers. Captain Haynes attempts to boost morale by providing free soft drinks and keeping the ship's "gedunk" (snack stand) open twenty-four hours a day, but the men still yearn for the ease of the four and twelve routine in their home port of San Diego. Besides, few of the younger officers and almost none of the enlisted men, it seems, share Captain Haynes' view that the *Providence,* lobbing an average of forty or fifty shells a day into Quang Tri province, is "here to see the war end honorably."

In the surrealistic half-light inside the six-inch gun turret, the sailors who load and ram the shells and powder reflect the underlying unease of the crew. "It's a rotten game, it's making no progress, it's just making people miserable," says Seaman Glenn Stillman, a bearded Mormon from Bountiful, Utah. Stillman, like most of the sailors, hopes that President Nixon's decision to mine all of North Vietnam's harbors will somehow shorten the war, but he is not optimistic. "He's made a decision forcing them to make a decision," he says, standing beside the gaping breach of an unloaded six-incher. "This war could build up any time."

The turret captain, standing by a phone near the entry to the turret, gets the order to load from the combat operations center. The bullet, or projectile, and powder casing arrive separately by hoist from below the gun. Stillman and another seaman pick the bullet from the hoist and place it in the breach. A third seaman then rams it into the gun itself by turning the switch on an electric hydraulic system. They follow precisely the same procedure as the powder casing emerges from below. Finally, the breach block closes and the petty officer in the combat operations center pulls a trigger that detonates the powder and fires the projectile.

Stillman complains somewhat querulously about his work. "It's too hot and I'm only getting five and a half hours sleep a day," he says. It is partly because the *Providence* is an old ship, commissioned at the Boston Naval Yard near the end of World War II, that it lacks the new machinery needed to transfer bullets and powder automatically from hoist to breach. When the ship was refitted in the late 1950s, it was provided with what her official history calls "the highly sophisticated and effective Terrier missile system and a nuclear capability." The history does not even mention her basic conventional weapons, admittedly less than entirely up to date.

Captain Haynes argues that the missile system, occupying the space of two gun turrets in the aft portion of the ship, "would be nice to have" for shooting down enemy aircraft, but no one seriously expects the opportunity to arise. (In any case, says one sailor, eight practice rounds fired by the missile system were all duds. Purse-lipped officers refuse to comment.) In the ward room, relaxing on sofas around a coffee table decked with *Life*s and *Business Week*s and *U.S. News and World Report*s, an intense, crew-cut lieutenant commander seriously criticizes the navy's failure to outfit its ships with enough of the newest, best guns.

"The United States is making a big mistake in not having more gunships," says the officer, who did a previous tour on a ship blockading the southern coast of Vietnam from enemy munitions traffic. "Take a look at these destroyer escorts we have around here," he says. "They have a single gun on some of them. If we're to have a navy and remain number one, we should have more ships with more guns." Another lieutenant commander admits the navy needs more ships to the job, but still praises the guns on the *Providence* for their accuracy. As evidence, he says that one of them "destroyed a truck today from ten miles."

How much do such little success stories really mean?

On the *Providence,* as in almost any other American military setting, the answers seem to vary according to rank and dedication to the service. At the apex of the pyramid on the *Providence,* Rear Admiral William Haley Rogers, commander of the entire "cruiser-destroyer flotilla" off Quang Tri, believes implicitly in the efficacy of shore bombardment. "Cruisers have large guns and are very good at it," says Admiral Rogers, a tall, swarthy man who wears a blue jacket with the emblems of a couple of his previous commands. "I can't think of anything more important than what we're doing now in terms of the defense of South Vietnamese cities south of Quang Tri."

Discussing the weapons at his disposal, Rogers talks as persuasively as an air force pilot advancing the need for bombing or an infantry commander explaining why you can't win a war without ground troops. It is up to young ensigns and lieutenants, few of whom plan to make a career in the navy, to point out some of the more obvious flaws in official logic. "Until a year ago we had the infantry over here and we didn't interdict enemy supply lines," says an ensign from upstate New York. "Now we're interdicting the supply lines but there's no infantry. If we'd done both at the same time, we might have won."

The crux of the ensign's argument is that mining the ports of North Vietnam will hardly win the war for South Vietnam if the South Vietnamese are incapable of fighting effectively on the ground. As for whether or not the shelling of Quang Tri province will permanently impede the flow of supplies farther south, the ensign assumes the question is meant as a joke and laughs good-naturedly in reply. "I guess the war will go on for another ten years," he says. "I happen to be rather conservative. I think we should have taken all these steps five years ago."

The lack of a real sense of purpose disturbs many sailors who might otherwise entirely favor the war. "I'm for fighting the war," says Signalman Third Class William

Dunn, a fair-haired Californian who's been on the ship for the past two years, "but I don't know if it's being fought right." As far as Dunn is concerned, the ship ought to have more raids like the one off Haiphong on May 10th nearly nineteen hours after President Nixon went on radio and television announcing that "all entrances to North Vietnamese ports will be mined to prevent access to these ports and North Vietnamese naval operations from these ports." Dunn, manning a telephone on the bridge of the *Providence,* knew the ship was heading toward Haiphong harbor when he spotted a beacon on a headland south of the entrance to the Red River channel.

"We weren't any farther out than maybe four miles," says Dunn. "I put everything together and figured we were making a raid on Haiphong." The *Providence,* all its lights out, was sailing full speed ahead, at approximately thirty knots, in a line with two other cruisers, the *Oklahoma City* and the *Newport News,* and two destroyers, the *Buchanan* and *Hanson.* "We saw a merchant ship lit up like a Christmas tree," says Dunn. "It began moving out to sea as we came in. All the lights inside the harbor were on, too. It looked like downtown LA." The North Vietnamese may have caught the cruiser-destroyer striking force on their radar, but basically the raid came as a surprise.

The ships, within 200 yards of the first buoys marking the channel, cut their speed to eighteen knots, turned, and then began firing broadside toward the shoreline. Four minutes later North Vietnamese coastal defense batteries began returning fire. "All you could hear was the whistle of the shells," says Signalman Apprentice Joseph Stankiewicz, who watched the engagement from the port side. "Then all the lights of the harbor went out at once." The battle, the first multicruiser strike since World War II, lasted only fifteen minutes, but it seemed much longer. "You could see these muzzle flashes on the beach," says Stankiewicz. "You get the feeling, if anything hits, it'll land in your lap."

The *Providence* fired some sixty rounds at a barracks complex, a fuel storage point, and some of the coastal defense sites. Then, still in line with the other ships, it turned, resumed full speed and left as quickly as it had come. Stankiewicz and Dunn heard some of the enemy shells landing in the water, but none of the ships was even scratched. "Everything was just fantastic," says Dunn. "It was the most beautiful operation I've ever seen. This ship just turned fantastically. I'm glad I got home to talk about it." The next day Captain Haynes went on the public address system to compliment and praise the crew. "You gotta be doing this for fun," he said, "because it's a crazy way to make a living."

Captain Haynes now tries to minimize the raid. "Just another fire mission," he says, but in retrospect its purpose appears to have been far more important than any of the men quite imagined at the time. The aim apparently was to soften North Vietnam's defenses before American planes began dropping the mines into the channel. "I wish John Wayne could have been there," says Quartermaster Third Class Steve V. Schlemmer, who admits having joined the navy "to get out of this stuff." Wayne "would have dug it," says Schlemmer. "Billy Graham could have been there beside him."

For the men of the *Providence,* the strike off Haiphong may well have been the climactic point of their tour. The ship, almost immediately after the raid, began sailing south and may remain here for some weeks. Without either the excitement, the tension, and danger of battle or some of the ease and amenities of home, as the officers are aware, men grow restive and unhappy, lax and lazy. "All we're doing now is banging holes in the land, making a few Olympic-sized swimming pools," says Schlemmer, whose father served as a navy aviation mechanic in World War II. "It's far enough where the guilt of killing people doesn't bother me, but it's still cutting into my sleep."

Not that shelling Quang Tri is entirely a one-sided proposition. Sometimes, particularly from around the mouth of the Cua Viet, a river ten miles south of the DMZ, enemy gunners have the temerity to fire back. The men on the deck wear flak jackets and helmets whenever the ship sails within ten miles of the Cua Viet, once a waterway for American vessels carrying supplies for bases near the DMZ. Living up to their reputation, the North Vietnamese fired some thirty rounds one day at the *Newport News* while it was shelling bunkers and storage depots of one kind or another around the Cua Viet. None of the enemy rounds found their mark that day, but shells have hit several destroyers over the past month.

Even this danger, however, may recede as North Vietnamese gunners begin to conserve their ammunition. Nor is there much chance that the cruisers will strike again at any of the North Vietnamese ports since they now run the danger of running over the mines. The only other possible threat may be that of Soviet minesweepers, accompanied by destroyers and cruisers, attempting to cut new channels into the ports. On the *Providence,* however, neither Admiral Rogers nor Captain Haynes regards this possibility at all seriously. "You could take any situation and postulate it," says Rogers, "but I can't think of anything that's occurred that would cause the Soviet Union to go to war. I don't think we've given them any reason to make a confrontation."

Assuming that Rogers is correct, then, one can only predict a long, dull tour for the men on the *Providence,* not to mention some 40,000 on the other sixty-four ships now cruising the waters off Vietnam with the rather large exception of the pilots flying from five different carriers. "It can be pretty miserable here," says Captain Haynes, "but we have a job to do." In the six-inch turret, Seaman Stillman agrees—and disagrees. "This is such a low level of human existence," he says. "I don't see why we should go on playing games like this."

Phnom Penh: August, 1973

They were two American adventurers, Don Douglass and Fred Compton, and they'd come to Cambodia in search of a war. They were pilots for an odd little company named Southeast Asian Air Transport, and they flew a lumbering old DC-4 approximately four times a day to a town named Kompong Cham, some fifty miles north of here on the Mekong. That is, they flew four flights a day when the ground crews weren't working very hard and didn't load or unload the plane quite fast enough. "Godammit, tomorrow we want to make five flights," growled Douglass, a one-time Massachusetts cop who had learned how to fly in his spare time. "We get paid a certain guarantee, and then we get more if we fly over a certain number of hours," he explained. "We don't like sitting around on the ground."

Douglass and Compton belonged to what you might call the hard-hat faction of the expatriate American set. They didn't really say so, but they clearly believed in fighting Communists. They thought bombing was a good thing, and they'd signed on with Southeast Asian Air Transport not only for the pay, which was high, but for the cause. "I want to help these people," said Douglass. "They're not gonna get anywhere without air power. I could do a lot of other things, but I like following the wars. I don't like your nine-to-five Stateside routine. I want something different." One could, if one wished, condemn Douglass on a number of different grounds, ranging from ignorance to insensitivity to worse, but somehow I found him more ingenuous than anything else. And I couldn't help but laugh—perhaps reflecting my own insensitivity—when he pleasantly told me exactly what he'd *really* like to do as long as he was in Cambodia.

"They've still got one old MIG-17 in their hangar over there," he confided. "The engine's out, but they're repairing it. I ran into the general of the Cambodian air force the other night—told him I'd be glad to fly it once they got it into shape." There was, it seemed, nothing that Douglass would not do with the MIG, the last of a squadron or so bequeathed the Cambodian government by the Soviet Union before the downfall of Prince Norodom Sihanouk in 1970. "Bombing, strafing, it's a lot of fun," said Douglass. "I flew a MIG in Nigeria in 1971. They bought it from the Egyptian government. The Russians were madder than hell about it, but there was nothing they could do. It took me five days to learn how to fly it, three days on the ground and two in the air." Compton, the captain on the DC-4, had yet to fly a MIG but was eager to learn. "They'd need another guy to fly it," he said. "Don could show me how. I'm ready. I'd do anything they wanted me to do with it. I think it'd be a real kick."

I'd met Don in the bar of the Monorom Hotel the day before. Relatively new to the war, he did not yet seem to harbor the anger of most pilots and contractors, not to mention CIA and State Department and military types, regarding the press. "Hey, I fly every day to Kompong Cham," he had told me. "Come out to the airport and take a ride in my plane." So I was in the jump seat, looking over their shoulders, as we circled the town. "We go around like this because the bad guys are out there," one of them explained. "We can't come in straight and low or they might take a shot at us." I'd been reading in Cambodian government handouts all about the bad guys outside Kompong Cham. They'd long since captured the road to Phnom Penh and just a couple of days previously had seized the town of Skoun, a bunkered, bombed-out enclave at a key junction. Now they were only a few miles away. I was anxious to get into Kompong Cham to do a story about a town under siege.

The apron by the airstrip was crowded with two or three transports when we landed. The civilian planes, such as the DC-4s owned by Southeast Asian Air Transport, carried in rice and other foodstuffs and left with tobacco or raw rubber, once shipped by highway or boat to Phnom

Penh. The military planes, notably a C-123 just turned over to the Cambodian air force by the United States, were hauling reinforcements for the town's defenses. Even so, one had difficulty conjuring a sense of real crisis. The few soldiers by the entrance to the airport lethargically waved almost anyone through the gate without bothering to check credentials. No bunkers were visible in the open green fields stretching beyond the road to a series of low-lying hills. "You think the enemy will attack?" I asked one of the soldiers through my interpreter, who had flown up in the same plane with me. "Our men are out there to stop them," the soldier replied, but I had the distinct sense the Khmer Rouge—"Red" Cambodian troops—could walk through the defenses like a sieve. A few mortar or rocket rounds could close the airport. Kompong Cham, population 80,000 or so, now swollen with refugees, lay like a ripe melon, ready to fall at the slightest pull.

"They can't hold it without bombing," one of the American pilots told me. "They may have to hire mercenary pilots—sign up Americans and buy some fighter planes and have them fight the war for them." The suggestion indicated the desperation of Cambodian government forces only a few days after the United States had finally ceased all bombing as a result of a rider on a congressional appropriations bill. The Khmer Rouge might not win in the first week, but they could quickly expand their control over the countryside, capturing towns and bases that had eluded them in more than three years of fighting since Sihanouk's downfall. Yet the town, when my interpreter and I finally got there after a five-mile ride in the early monsoon rain, did not seem to have changed much since I had last been there, two years ago. Old French-built cars and Japanese motor scooters and American-made military vehicles still rolled leisurely down the broad, tree-shaded streets. The governor's mansion remained as a symbol of power and security in the center of a gray-green-brownish kind of park. The general, at that particular moment, was conferring with some aides, but he was glad to talk to me.

"The enemy came from the highlands, like the water coming from the higher to the lower region," he remarked, as the rain poured down on the roof. "There are enemy troops, but we have stopped them in many places. They cannot attack us." What if they hit the airfield—the only entry for all the necessities of war and daily life now that both the road and river routes were closed? "Around the airfield, there are no houses or villages," said the general, with the social ease and glibness that somehow seem to characterize all senior Cambodian officials, nurtured on French colonialism and the postcolonial social milieu of the capital. "If the enemy comes near the air field," he explained, "we can use our air strikes," as delivered by the Cambodian air force's newly acquired T-28s. The general was unfailingly courteous, but his briefing was pathetically similar to dozens of conversations I have had with Cambodian officers over the past few years. One only had to talk to people around the town to confirm an initial impression of military weakness and ineptitude.

"They overran three positions two miles from here last night," said a merchant sipping thick coffee in a little café in the center of town. "We don't think there are enough soldiers to defend us. If they keep on attacking, the enemy will easily get into town and we will have to run away." The coffee shop was crowded with tradesmen, clerks, bureaucrats, and young officers. They were still there, in Kompong Cham, because they had no way to get out, no place to go, no exit. They listened and smiled and joked about our conversation. If the town were in danger, you couldn't tell it from the expressions on their faces. But Cambodia is that way. You never know, when you encounter troops in the field, if they feel they are under pressure or not unless the bullets and shells are actually flying. And even then you can't be entirely sure. A few hundred meters behind the front lines you are quite likely to see soldiers lolling in hammocks or chatting and joking as if the war were a hundred miles away. It was the same way in Kompong Cham that day—except that the scene, if anything, was more relaxed, almost charming, as the rain gradually stopped and the sun filtered through the haze.

I'd originally thought of staying overnight in the governor's mansion, at the invitation of the general, but by late afternoon I thought I had gleaned about as much from Kompong Cham as my readers would care to know. My interpreter and I found the same motorbike-taxi driver who had met us at the airport and drove out of town on the same tranquil road, weaving our way around occasional bicycles and bullock carts, grinning at peasant farmers who grinned back at us with open, typically Cambodian countenances. It was the end of the working day at the textile factory, and we were caught for a moment in a wave of small vehicles of varying descriptions, but the road was soon quiet again, and my interpreter asked me if I would like to see the ancient temple complex before turning down the last stretch toward the airport. "It is as old as Angkor Wat," he assured me. "Maybe you won't have another chance to see it again." The driver veered onto a mud road, past some crumbling, blackened walls, then under an arch and around a large pond. The ruins, perhaps somewhat restored but never rebuilt as completely as the temples in the Angkor region, rose mysteriously beyond thatched peasant homes. We didn't have time to stop and look as we might have wished. We wanted to reach the airstrip in time for Don and Fred's last run back to Phnom Penh. Besides, there would always be another chance, another trip. The ruins could wait.

But we were wrong. The ruins couldn't wait. Three or four days later the Khmer Rouge did what everyone except the general had anticipated. They rocketed and closed the airport. Then they advanced on the ground, overrunning the factory and the temple area and a university campus, also near the airport. They overran outpost after outpost until the Cambodian defenders, reinforced the day we were there by two fresh battalions, controlled only the center of the city and still couldn't prevent infiltrators from exploding grenades in the market and sniping at the governor's mansion. Cambodian T-28s bombed and strafed, but they could hardly replace the American F-4s and B-52s on which Cambodian commanders had always depended to postpone their final defeat. Don and Fred had to fly their DC-4 elsewhere. American military planes were airdropping supplies over the center of the city. No more easy milkruns for eager young pilots out to see the war. Nor did I hear anything about the last MIG-17 in the Cambodian air force. I assume it's still in the hangar, where it may form the nucleus of the next Cambodian air force if Prince Sihanouk returns to power.

chapter 6:

"Such a nice man"

Others also served. They weren't exactly soldiers. Nor were they militia or "people's self-defense force" types. They were generally described, for want of any better term, as "paramilitary." They were all over Indochina, on all sides of the conflict, but the most famous were the "advisers" and what-not hired by the Central Intelligence Agency to run the war in Laos. They had no precedent in American history, these daring, often middle-aged men in PX sports shirts and slacks, who had learned their trade while in the army's special forces or the marine corps, among other places. They theoretically did not carry weapons, but naturally they thought nothing of breaking this rule while training hardy tribesmen, jumping with them into combat, and spending weeks in some of Indochina's densest jungles or scaling its craggiest peaks.

If the CIA in Laos had any equal, it was the CIA's Phoenix program in Vietnam. There, CIA agents not only encouraged the Vietnamese to coordinate and pool the intelligence-gathering efforts of various agencies but also schooled them in the recondite arts of intimidation and torture. (The CIA in Vietnam, incidentally, didn't really approve of straight killing. "The dead don't talk," CIA people reminded the Vietnamese, who were sometimes overly anxious to do away with their victims in the process of torturing them.) The Phoenix operation in Vietnam, however, was the brainchild and plaything of button-down bureaucrats, notably the cool, taciturn William Colby, rewarded in 1973 with the post of director of the entire agency.

For real romance, for adventure that was stranger than fiction but for some reason was never made into a movie or television serial, you couldn't beat the secret war in Laos. One of the most colorful warriors in this struggle was a tough guy named Tony Poe. I never met him, which is just as well, because Tony was madder than hell at me after my article about him finally appeared. "And when Tony gets mad . . ." one of my informants reminded me, leaving the rest of the sentence ominously unspoken.

Bangkok: June, 1971

He's a round-faced, cheery man with a cherubic smile and a charming family. He's a satanic killer with a glowering sneer and a penchant for preserving the ears of his victims in formaldehyde. He's a classic Dr. Jekyll-and-Mister Hyde, and he's been waging the most secret phase of America's secret war in Southeast Asia for the past ten years.

He's just plain Tony Poe to the boys at the Napoleon Café and the Derby King on Bangkok's Patpong Road, a watering ground for Air America pilots, CIA types, journalists, and other assorted Indochinese hands, but his real name's Anthony A. Poshepny. He's a refugee from Hungary, an ex-marine who fought on Iwo Jima, and a dedicated patriot of his adopted land, the United States of America, for which he's risked his life on literally hundreds of occasions while ranging through the undulating velvet-green crags and valleys of China, Laos, and Thailand.

He also shuns publicity and *hates* reporters, as I discovered in a month-long search for him beginning in the Thai capital of Bangkok and extending to the giant American airbases in northeastern Thailand and to the mountains of northern Laos. The search for Tony Poe ended where it had begun, in the lobby of the Amarin Hotel, a luxury lodging run by the Imperial Hotel of Tokyo, on Bangkok's Ploenchit Road, a six-lane-wide avenue jammed with traffic running from dawn to dusk through a residential and shopping district supported largely by rich American "farangs" (the slightly demeaning Thai term for "foreigners"). There, before leaving Bangkok for the last time, I picked up a note, signed simply "Tony" in a flowing scrawl, stating that he had to decline my request for an interview. "I beelieve [sic] that you can appreciate my reason for not seeking public commentary," wrote Tony in formal-statement style befitting a public official—and obviously suggested, if not dictated, by one of his superiors with the Central Intelligence Agency.

"C-I-A?" asked the cute little Japanese girl at the desk of the Amarin, carefully enunciating each of the letters, smiling slightly with glittering white teeth, and raising her eyebrows flirtatiously. "Oh, no," she said, raising her left hand to cover the shy smile. "Tony Poe is airplane pilot. He works for Continental Air Services. You mean Continental, not CIA?" An assistant manager, also Japanese, showed me the card Tony had signed only a few days before my arrival at the Amarin, in mid-1971, at the beginning of my search for him. Tony, it seemed, generally stayed at the Amarin, only a few blocks from the modernesque American embassy on a tree-shaded street off Ploenchit Road. He was a familiar, beloved character to the staff at the Amarin—the opposite of his public image as a sinister, secret killer and trainer of anti-Communist guerrilla warriors.

"Anthony A. Poshepny," read the top line. "Air Ops Officer—Continental Air Services." So Tony, with a record of more combat jumps than any other American civilian in Indochina, had used Continental as his "cover" while training doughty mountain tribesmen to fight against regular Communist troops advancing year-by-year from both China and North Vietnam. The revelation of Tony's cover surprised me since I had assumed he would declare himself a bona fide U.S. government official—perhaps an adviser to border patrol police units, the traditional cover under which CIA operatives masquerade in both Thailand and Laos. Nonetheless, Continental was a logical choice. Like Air America, Continental regularly ferries men and supplies to distant outposts throughout Indochina.

The next two lines on the form were even more revealing, in terms of what Poshepny was doing at the present. Following "Going To," Tony had written, "Udorn," the name of the base town in northeastern Thailand from which the United States not only flies bombing runs over all of Laos but also coordinates the guerrilla war on the ground. And where was Tony "Coming From"? According to the form, his origin was Phitsanulok, a densely jungled mountain province famed in Thailand for incessant fighting between Communist-armed guerrillas, most of them members of mountain tribes, and ill-trained Thai army soldiers and policemen. Tony, it seemed, sometimes vanished into the wilds of Phitsanulok, where the jungle was so thick and the slopes so steep as to discourage the toughest American advisers, on a mysterious training venture not even known to most American officials with top-secret security clearances, much less to the girls behind the desk of the Amarin.

"Oh, he's such a nice man," one of the Japanese girls

assured me when I asked how she liked Tony, who, I'd been warned by other journalists, might be inclined to shoot on sight any reporter discovered snooping too closely into his past—or present. "He has a very nice wife and three lovely children," the girl burbled on, pausing to giggle slightly between phrases. "He comes here on vacation from up-country." The impression Poshepny had made on the girls at the Amarin was a tribute both to his personality and his stealth. In fact, as I discovered while tracing him from the south of Thailand to northern Laos, he already had an opulent home in Udorn for his wife, a tribal princess whom he had married a year or so ago. Mrs. Poshepny, a tiny, quick-smiling girl whom Tony had met while training members of the Yao tribe for special missions into China, liked to come to Bangkok for shopping while Tony conferred with his CIA associates on the guarded third floor, the CIA floor, of the American embassy.

It was highly ironic that I should have learned that Tony stayed at the Amarin while in Bangkok, for it was only by chance that I had checked in there at the beginning of my search—and only during small talk with the desk clerks that I found one of Tony's registration cards. The day after my arrival in Bangkok local journalists gave me my first inkling of some of the rumors surrounding Tony Poe. One of them, named Lance Woodruff, formerly a reporter on one of Bangkok's two English-language newspapers, now with the Asian Institute of Technology in Bangkok, said Poe not only hated reporters but had been known to "do away with people he doesn't like." Woodruff compared Poe to a figure from "Terry and the Pirates" and told me the story of how Poe lined one wall of a house in northern Laos, near the Chinese border, with heads of persons whom he had killed. None of the contacts whom I met in Bangkok had the slightest clue as to Tony's whereabouts—except that he was somewhere "up country" training tribesmen to fight the Communists, possibly in China itself.

Still unaware that Poe stayed at the Amarin, I drove to a town named Ubon, some 350 miles northeast of Bangkok and 200 miles southeast of Udorn. My hunch, based only on a tip supplied by a former Peace Corps girl whom I had met in Saigon, was that Poe was training tribesmen from the Bolovens Plateau in southern Laos to fight against North Vietnamese troops expanding base areas following the South Vietnamese army's assault across the Laotian frontier several months earlier. At Ubon, in hopes of falling into conversations with pilots who might know Tony, I visited the air base, similar to that at Udorn, from which American warplanes fly on daily bombing and strafing runs over southern Laos. Although newsmen are banned from the base, ostensibly commanded by the Thai government, unless they have special, almost impossible to obtain permission from Thai authorities, I got on by flashing a Department of Defense card routinely issued reporters in South Vietnam.

The air base at Ubon was as neat and well-manicured as a suburban American country club. Enlisted airmen strolled casually in Bermuda shorts and sports shirts purchased at the base exchange, while off-duty pilots chatted amiably in the officers' clubs. No one, it seemed, had ever heard of Poe, but an officer in an army special forces unit on the base suggested I talk to one or two American civilian advisers, presumably CIA men operating under the cover of the U.S. Operations Mission. Neither was in when I called, so I hired a taxi and drove some fifty miles to the Laotian frontier. It occurred to me I could learn still more by visiting the town of Pakse, twenty miles beyond the border, across the mile-wide Mekong River. Pakse was not only the leading center in southern Laos but the headquarters for all operations aimed at staunching the North Vietnamese offensive in that region.

It seemed indicative of the government's desire to conceal Poshepny's activities that one of the American refugee advisers, who might himself have been with the CIA, advised me that Tony was "off Florida looking for sunken treasure." None of the other American officials in Pakse volunteered even that much information. The North Vietnamese had just overrun a town some thirty miles to the east, and the wives and families of all Americans in Pakse had been evacuated to the Laotian capital of Vientiane, a pleasant oasis still secure from war. Since the Americans were in no mood to entertain a reporter, I found a military telephone and called one of the CIA men whose name I had obtained on the airbase at Ubon. The spook, named Larry Waters, who had the title of public safety adviser for the Ubon region, told me that Tony had recently been released from a hospital in Bangkok after a grenade had exploded in a training accident, blowing two fingers off his left hand.

It was not until reaching Vientiane, however, that I obtained my first real break on Poe's whereabouts. At the Settha Palace, a graceful colonial-style hotel on a tree-shaded street opposite the embassy of Communist China, I met the manager and part-owner, Bob Violet, a balding, one-time administrative officer of the American embassy. After congratulating Violet on the decor of the bar, much improved since I first stayed in the hotel in 1966, I asked him what had happened to Tony. Violet explained that "most of those guys have gone to Thailand." Among them, he said, were Jack Shirley (once stationed at the top-secret American base at Long Cheng, south of the Plain of Jars in northern Laos) and Sam Hopler and a man known only as Zeke—two other old Laos hands. All of them were known to hang out at the bars on Patpong Road in Bangkok when not at their desks in the embassy. They often weekended, said Violet, at an island off the town of Huahin in southern Thailand.

Wherever else Poe might be found, he apparently was no longer in Laos, from which he had sent tribesmen on missions as far as 200 miles into the mountains of Yunnan Province in southwestern China. I visited a site for refugees driven from their homes on the Plain of Jars eighty miles north of Vientiane, where refugee workers said they hadn't seen him for at least a year. One of them, a male nurse named Jack Thiel employed by the American aid mission, recalled that Tony periodically visited that site and another at Sam Thong, finally overrun by North Vietnamese troops in March of 1970, but then seemed to have vanished. "He was a tough-looking guy with a red face, a powerful build, about five feet ten inches tall," said Thiel as we sat in the small operating room of the American-run medical facility, the only one in the region for several hundred thousand refugees created by the combination of American bombing and North Vietnamese offensives.

Other refugee workers, even some who had been in Laos for a number of years, were equally vague as to Tony's activities, The reason, of course, was that they would lose their jobs if it were discovered that they had revealed what Tony had done. However, a young American reporter, Michael Morrow of Dispatch News Service, had already "blown Tony's cover"—a factor that accounted in part for Poe's leaving Laos and shifting his operations to Thailand. "Poe is a legendary figure in Laos," wrote Morrow, a radical journalist who later was expelled from South Vietnam for his dealings with pro-Communist politicians. "He is an ex-marine noncommissioned officer, wounded in landing at Iwo Jima, who remained in Asia after World War II. In the '50s he helped organize Tibetan CIA-aided insurgents, escorted them to Colorado for training, and finally went back with them to Tibet."

Morrow, whose article appeared in the San Francisco *Chronicle,* Boston *Globe,* and a number of other papers in September, 1970, noted that Poe was "known best for his dislike of journalists, disregard for orders and radio codes, capacity for Lao whiskey, and expertise at clandestine guerrilla operations." The American press attache in Vientiane, Andy Guzowski, a captain in the Polish navy in

World War II, smilingly showed me a copy of Mike's article and claimed that Poe had left Laos in July of 1970, before it appeared in print. In fact, as I discovered in Vientiane, the article provided the new American ambassador to Laos, a tough "field marshal" type with the blueblood name of G. McMurtie Godley, with the perfect excuse for having Tony removed from Laos to Thailand.

"Tony was acting like the king of his own kingdom," said a vociferous acquaintance of his whom I encountered in one of those Vientiane bars habituated by Air America pilots, marine guards with the U.S. embassy, and others somehow associated with the outsized American community in the lotus-land capital. "He thought he'd been there so long he could defy the ambassador." Godley, a silver-haired patrician who's previously served as ambassador to the Congo, is, if anything, as hawkish as Poe in his attitude toward the Communists. He personally recommended escalation of American bombing of North Vietnamese troop concentrations in 1969 and 1970, a decision that not only created thousands of new refugees but also, according to interviews with some of them, resulted in needless deaths of civilians and destruction of their homes.

Why, then, was Godley eager for an excuse to get rid of Poe, a man who had risked his life on hundreds of occasions while he, Godley, savored the ambassadorial comforts of an air-conditioned office complex, residence and limousine? The answer may be that Tony was so experienced in his work that he viewed Godley as an outside amateur whose orders and advice need not be seriously regarded. Godley, while he respected Tony's ability and courage, is the kind of man who demands complete loyalty from all his subordinates, and he was enraged by the specter of a CIA person who looked down on him professionally and preferred to operate independently. Tony, in fact, had just grown too cocky. He was, after all, the senior CIA man in northwestern Laos, near the sensitive tri-border of Burma, Laos, and

China, and he had helped to organize an entire army of Meo tribesmen in the early 1960s. This army, although decimated and demoralized by a series of North Vietnamese offensives, provided the last defense for northern Laos—and Vientiane itself.

It was not, however, the North Vietnamese but the Chinese whom Tony really hated the most. It was apparently during his early experience flying with anti-Communist guerrillas into Tibet that Poshepny began to focus his hatred almost exclusively on the Chinese regime, whose troops had overrun Tibet shortly after their rise to power in Peking in 1949. After the United States had officially given up the salvation of Tibet as a lost cause, Poe was a frequent visitor to a camp known as "Little Switzerland," on the Mekong River several miles after it tumbles out of China. Little Switzerland was perhaps the most clandestine, most vital CIA listening post for all of China except for well-known, nonsecret facilities in the British Crown Colony of Hong Kong and on the island of Taiwan, occupied by the American-supported Nationalist Chinese regime. Finally, several years ago, Tony succeeded Bill Young, the son of a missionary in northern Thailand, in the top CIA position for northwestern Laos.

It was during this period that the legend of Tony Poe began to grow. He was said to dislike all non-CIA Americans, even those working for the government, and to have threatened to kill unwelcome visitors who wandered into his secret headquarters at Nam Yu, the village near the Chinese border from which he sent fifteen-man teams into China, according to Morrow, "to tap Chinese telegraph lines, watch roads, and do other types of intelligence gathering." The tri-border region was also the center of the opium trade, from which both Lao officials and a horde of Nationalist Chinese troops, driven from China in 1949, reaped enormous profits. Although Tony knew all about the opium trade, he preferred to avoid it, to forget it, while pursuing his own ends against the Communist Chinese, who had sent some ten thousand army engineers into northern Laos to build a road complex stretching from North Vietnam to northern Thailand. Neither Laos nor the United States wanted to risk head-on war with China by destroying the road system, but Tony's tribesmen kept careful watch on what was happening.

Tony was so engrossed in his work that he learned the language of the Yao, the second most important tribe after the Meo, so well as to converse fluently in it and not reveal his identity as an American in conversations over the radio with agents deep inside China. The Yao were said to revere him as almost a godlike figure, one of many deities embraced by their animist cult.

Insatiably cruel in battle, Tony also was unbelievably brave. Jumping into combat with his tribal guerrillas, he was wounded a dozen times. There was always, however, more to Tony Poe than blood-and-guts combat, as was revealed in his romance with the daughter of one of the Yao tribal leaders. Although it is not known what she thought of the ears of victims that Tony kept in pickle jars, she lived with him for a number of years in several of his jungle hideaways. Tony and the girl might have been content with this relationship, but the American embassy in Vientiane strongly urged they get married after local politicians began commenting on the fact that they had brought out-of-wedlock children into the world. "It was a shotgun wedding," confided one of the gossips at the White Rose, a Vientiane bar noted for bar girls who perform impromptu stripteases at a dollar a dance. "But it was still true love," my source insisted, and it also qualified Tony's wife and family for the perquisites and benefits of official American "dependents," including the home at Udorn.

The talk at the Vientiane bars, in fact, was that Poshepny was connected with air operations at the American air base at Udorn, forty miles to the south of

Vientiane, rather than at Ubon, as I had first supposed. Armed with this tip, I crossed the Mekong back to Thailand and hired a local taxi for the drive to Udorn. Flashing my Department of Defense card to get on this base, also ordinarily closed to newsmen, I went to the airmen's club nearest the entrance to make some phone calls. Since I still didn't know that Tony was covered by Continental, I called Air America and spoke to a man who identified himself as Bill Yarborough. This man said he not only knew Tony Poe but had seen him a few days ago and suggested I call customer air operations, for which he gave me the phone number.

At air ops a man with a Thai accent answered the phone. "Where's Tony?" I asked. "No here, he no here one week," was the reply, approximately. "Where's he at?" I asked again, attempting to sound like a pilot or young GI. "Up north," answered the Thai, evidently employed as a clerk. "North what?" I asked, since I still wasn't certain whether he was in northern Laos or northern Thailand. "Near Chieng Mai," was the reply. Chieng Mai, it happens, is the leading town of northern Thailand and a cultural center famed for its temples and art. Sensing that I was getting closer to my goal, I asked the Thai what Tony was doing up there. Where, exactly, could I find him? "He at Phitcamp 603," I was told. "What's that?" I asked. "Phitcamp 603," the Thai repeated. Then *he* had a couple of questions. "Why you want to know? Who are you?" I gave my name over the phone—didn't want to be accused of misidentifying myself if an investigation were to ensue. The Thai asked where I was. "At one of the clubs," I replied, over the noise of a jukebox in the background.

The Thai voice then went off the line, and a peculiar buzzing filled the void. My feeling was the phone was being tapped or, at any rate, a tracer was on the call. I hung up, walked off the base and took the night train, one hour later, to Bangkok. No one had yet apprised me of Poe's bond with

Continental, but I had discovered what might be of greater importance: the precise code number of the camp in Phitsanulok province from which he was then operating.

Although I now had a fair idea of Poe's whereabouts, I still hadn't seen him. After arriving in Bangkok, I checked in again at the Amarin Hotel and then went to the Derby King, one of the bars where Tony's friends hung out. The only person at the bar, it happened, was a paunchy, balding American named Stan Griffin, who said he ran a travel agency but seemed to know Tony and Jack and Zeke and Sam, the boys who worked for "the agency" (not Stan's "travel agency," but the CIA). It turned out that Jack Shirley, Tony's real boss with the American embassy in Bangkok, was weekending by the beach at Huahin in southern Thailand, but Stan told me all about the "accident" in which Tony had lost two fingers on his left hand a couple of months previously. It seemed Tony had been teaching some Thai police recruits how to defuse a grenade and it had exploded, killing one of the Thai and wounding Tony. Stan said that Tony had been wounded six times already. "It figures that Tony got out of that scrape," he observed, slowly stirring his drink in the half-light of the bar. "He was so damned lucky, he'd get out of anything."

A couple of days later, at Napoleon's, next door to the Derby King, I met Sam—Sam Hopler—a handsome, clean-cut type, straight out of Hollywood, with distinguished-looking gray hair, a pleasant manner, and an open personality. Sam suggested I leave a note for Tony in care of Jack—Jack Shirley, whose offices were on the third floor of the embassy. "Does Tony get down to Bangkok much?" I asked Sam. "He was just here," Sam replied. "He generally stays at the Amarin" (the hotel at which, by complete coincidence, I was also accustomed to staying). It was after returning to the Amarin that afternoon that I discovered that Anthony Poshepny had checked in—and out—while I was looking for him in Laos and northeastern Thailand.

Picking up his full Hungarian name and his affiliation with Continental from the registration card, I wrote him a long letter, in care of Jack Shirley, requesting an interview. "My aim is not to 'expose' your activities," I wrote, "but to chronicle the lifestyle of an individual who has led a fascinating, exciting career on an assignment little known or appreciated by the American public." I left the note with the marine guard at the American embassy, who immediately called a secretary on the third floor, who came downstairs to get it and deliver it to Shirley.

While awaiting my reply I also spoke to a young foreign service officer assigned to the embassy's counter-insurgency section, superficially not run by the CIA but obviously a cover for CIA operatives. The official provided me with nonclassified information I already knew about Communist guerrilla activities in the northern provinces of Thailand. He noted that Thai police had some training camps in that region and that the U.S. Operations Mission participated in this program in strictly an advisory capacity. Since it was well-known that the CIA in Thailand often shields its activities behind the USOM police advisory effort, I then asked what Tony Poe was doing in Phitsanulok province.

The official said he had never heard of anyone by that name and continued to plead ignorance after I had given him Poe's full, original Hungarian name and the name and number of the training camp where he worked. It was clear from the official's studied nonreaction that he was entirely familiar with Tony Poe's activities. This realization was underlined by his reply to my comment that it seemed rather fantastic that a wandering American reporter such as myself could find all this top-secret information without any kind of security clearance. That, said the official, was "a question that one might well ask" and to which he too would like some kind of reply. Still, he insisted he had never heard of Poe and suggested I obtain formal permission from Thai authorities to visit one of the police training camps if I were interested in that particular program.

The Thai, of course, would keep me away from Phitcamp 603 and send me somewhere else, to some showplace for visitors. When I pointed out this reality to the official, he asked me whether or not I was certain that Poe, "if he exists," was performing any kind of training function on behalf of the Thai. The question helped confirm my suspicion that Poe, after leaving Laos, continued to train mountain tribesmen—for the fighting not in Thailand, but in Laos. Since Poe spoke at least one, possibly more, tribal languages, it seemed more than likely the CIA would want him to deal with the same people even if he were no longer in Laos. In order to throw me off the search, the American official emphasized the point that Poe might have no connection with the training of Thai police, but his question had quite the opposite effect. "That's entirely your speculation," he said, rather impatiently, when I told him bluntly that I could tell from what he said that Poe was training tribesmen at a camp in Thailand supposedly set up for training Thai police recruits, but actually used for quite another purpose.

The reason for the sensitivity of Americans on this subject is obvious. The United States does not want enemy forces, including propagandists, to know the full extent of its role in Laos, already publicized by hearings before Senator Fulbright's Senate subcommittee on foreign relations. The Geneva agreement of 1962 specifically forbids the introduction of foreign troops into Laos, a condition flagrantly violated by all participants in the war. Another reason for sensitivity is the reluctance of Thailand to publicize its own role in the war. This reluctance (or embarrassment) accounts for the difficulties encountered by newsmen in obtaining permission to visit Thai air bases, from which U.S. warplanes fly missions over Laos and Cambodia. Thailand welcomes American military assistance but wants to keep an appearance, as much as possible, of independence from overwhelming American influence.

In view of the official desire for secrecy, it seemed unlikely that I would learn anything more at the American embassy. Instead, I went to Singapore, the bustling island-nation to the south of Thailand, to meet two journalists who knew about Poe—Mike Morrow and Sterling Seagrave, the son of the famed "Burma Surgeon," glorified in book and movie. Morrow, who had gone to Singapore after his expulsion from South Vietnam, described Poe as "extremely dangerous." He said that his article about him had resulted in a complete investigation in which Richard Helms, the head of the CIA, had visited Vientiane (while on a trip primarily to South Vietnam) to find out the source of the leak. Seagrave claimed that Helms had read Poe the riot act for ever letting anyone know about his activities. After Helms' visit, Ambassador Godley, who wanted Poe out of Laos under any circumstances, had no difficulty persuading the CIA to keep him in Thailand.

"It was kind of a blow to Tony," said one of his friends on Patpong Road. "Since the Morrow story appeared, he hates reporters as much as he does Communists." It was rather surprising to me, in fact, that Poe even bothered to write a note turning down my request for an interview, but it was awaiting me in a small envelope at the desk of the Amarin when I got back from Singapore. It had no dateline other than "Thailand" in the top right-hand corner and no signature other than "Tony," but I was sure of its authenticity. The handwriting was the same kind of scrawl that I had seen on the registration card. I was sure, after all I had heard about Poe, that he meant what he said—that he would not submit to an interview or even a face-to-face meeting but preferred to remain a faceless legend, even if he could never return to the jungles of Laos and China, where he'd operated in complete secrecy for so many years.

Since Tony's transfer to Thailand, he's suffered even more as a result of the vicissitudes of American foreign policy. President Nixon's decision to attempt to restore some level of relations between Washington and Peking has forced the United States to curtail, if not completely cancel, all its secret missions across the Chinese border. Tony's Yao guerrillas must operate exclusively in Laos, and perhaps Burma and Thailand. For old CIA hands, the prospect of rapprochement with China represents the destruction of all their efforts for the past generation. "Nixon's gone soft on Communism like all the rest of them," observed a tough-looking, ruddy type over his beer. "Pretty soon we'll have to clear out of this whole area."

The change in American policy may mean the end of the era that Tony, in secret, came to symbolize. While the United States is softening its outlook toward China, Anthony Poshepny and some of his confreres are quietly looking forward to retirement in homes on the white sandy beaches of southern Thailand, overlooking the Gulf of Siam. "Zeke, Sam, Jack—they're all gone now," said one of the old hands in Vientiane. "But they'll never leave Asia. They'll still be around talking about the good old days when we were fighting the commies like we should, or almost. They were a tough crowd, those boys, the toughest of the tough. They were the side of the war that nobody knew, not even those pinko Senate investigators."

chapter 7:

"La guerre populaire"

The sense of disillusionment was universal among anti-Communist forces in Indochina, but there were variations. The Cambodians had their own special approach to the conflict. When it all began in Cambodia, after the overthrow of Prince Norodom Sihanouk on March 18, 1970, while he was visiting Moscow en route to Peking, Cambodians responded as if they were going to a party, or, at any rate, a crusade. They patriotically rallied, held demonstrations, climbed on Pepsi-Cola trucks and a melange of other conveyances, and went down the roads in search of the enemy. The frivolity, the fatal gaiety of the Cambodian approach was permanently embedded in my consciousness when I joined a Cambodian general on "La Guerre Populaire," an upper-class effort to inspire the peasantry with a sense of loyalty.

The general, as the real war worsened, was rewarded for his easygoing incompetence, his cunning, and his corruption by a promotion and reassignment to Phnom Penh as commander-in-chief of the entire Cambodian army. The peasants, whose loyalty the government never did win, either sided with the Khmer Rouge or fled to the relative safety in Phnom Penh as the war spread over the countryside and the Americans bombed in support of Cambodian troops. The students and bureaucrats, anti-Sihanoukist at the outset, displayed varying degrees of lethargy or nostalgia for the Sihanouk era while the government in Phnom Penh bumbled through incessant political and military crises.

The Cambodian soldiers in the field never seemed to learn to fight the war no matter how much time they spent at it. Whenever I saw them, more than two years after my excursion with the general, they were sleeping or cooking when they should have been advancing. They rarely prepared more than flimsy barbed-wire defenses, and they clung to the main roads and villages while the Khmer Rouge swept around them, set up ambushes and infiltrated government-controlled areas. The basic image of the Cambodian army, as I witnessed it in 1971, remained constant despite massive infusions of American aid, air strikes and training. As the corrupt general, imitating the French, might have said, *"Plus ça change, plus c'est la même chose",* The more it changes, the more it stays the same.

Phnom Penh: April, 1971

The high command in the yellow building on one of the capital's widest French-designed boulevards had launched what is called "la guerre populaire." With my interpreter, a student of ancient Khmer inscriptions, I dutifully drove out of Phnom Penh in a Mercedes-Benz taxi, past the charred remains of military structures near the airport and on to a town named Kompong Speu, some forty miles down the highway. The skeletal frames of old buildings reminded us of a series of battles for the town some months ago, but the war today was off the main road. Jumping into a Russian-built military truck, we rode down a dirt track from which tiny particles of red dust billowed furiously behind the wheels of dilapidated buses, Land Rovers and new American-supplied jeeps.

Ten miles south of Kompong Speu we met the regional commander, Brigadier General Sosthene Fernandez, sitting under a green canvas tent labeled, "Relief Supplies from the Government of New Zealand." General Fernandez, a short, compact man with a crewcut, deprecating smile and deep-set, almost pleading eyes, waved us to seats across an improvised table made of boards and crates. Beside him were his senior subalterns, Colonel Ung Than, the provincial governor, a rotund civilian who confessed he only wore his military reserve uniform "pour l'opération," and Colonel Norodom Chantarangsey, a brigade commander and wealthy member of one of Cambodia's two principal royal families.

"Our life is happy because we can share equally," said General Fernandez, pointing toward bottles of cognac and whiskey and steaming plates of fish, pork, beef and rice, surrounded by side dishes of vegetables and sauces. "La guerre populaire," it was clear from first glance around the general's "forward headquarters," set at the base of a couple of knolls on which soldiers were mounting small outposts, was a grand picnic in which all members of the general's following in Kompong Speu were deployed on a two-day holiday before returning to more humdrum chores. "This is the first time we make such popular war with villagers, monks, military, civilians, young and old," Fernandez explained while offering succulent pieces of sausage to his guests. "Those who have no rifles, who are not military, can come with canes and knives because we are one-minded against the enemy."

"La guerre populaire," as waged during our excursion with General Fernandez' troops south of Kompong Speu, typified Cambodian military operations I witnessed in a month of travels around the country. There was the momentary flush of enthusiasm of students and teachers, freed for two days from classes in town to propagandize among the peasantry. There was the military ineptitude of the troops, who rarely patrolled far beyond main roads, did little more than guard stationary outposts at night, and were powerless to provide real protection against roving bands of Viet Cong or North Vietnamese soldiers supported by more indigenous Cambodian guerrillas than officers in Phnom Penh cared to admit. Finally, there was the overpowering sense of privilege, of condescension mingled with cynicism exuded by senior Cambodian officers, few of whom had really had to fight seriously before the overthrow of Prince Norodom Sihanouk on March 18th of last year.

"It's remarkable how much this army has improved," runs the cliché of diplomats and military attachés assigned to the burgeoning American Embassy, expanded from a dozen to nearly a hundred men in the twelve months. The main improvements, however, are quantitative rather than qualitative. The army, operating with a steady flow of American arms and ammunition ferried up the Mekong River or flown aboard American or South Vietnamese cargo planes from South Vietnam, still controls little more than a third of the country, mainly the heartland around the capital of Phnom Penh. North Vietnamese forces seized most of the northern and northeastern provinces shortly after Sihanouk's fall and also range virtually unopposed, except by American air strikes, across the mountains south of the capital. South Vietnamese troops, whom most Cambodians regard with the same hatred with which they view the Vietnamese Communists, have secured some of the border regions and may well insist on holding them even if the Cambodian government asks them to leave.

After more than a year of warfare, in fact, the hold of the government over even the center of the country is so tenuous that American officers admit privately the Communists "could overrun Phnom Penh any time they want." North Vietnamese sappers dramatized this point by a raid on the airport, in which they adroitly knocked out more than thirty planes and helicopters, burned military barracks and hangars, and damaged meteorological and radar equipment before Cambodian guards could begin to respond. Intelligence experts estimate at least a thousand Communist "troops"—including saboteurs, spies and propagandists—are permanently in the capital, defended by 45,000 men, roughly a quarter of the government's army. Phnom Penh's best defense, however, probably lies in the reality that North Vietnam does not seem to want the city while attempting to solidify positions in the countryside.

"The Communist strategy is to try to restrict the government pretty much to the environs of the city but not to take it over," observed an experienced diplomat here. "The North Vietnamese would find Phnom Penh much too difficult to govern if they actually held it. They'd have to set up an entire satellite regime. They might bring Sihanouk back from Peking, but it's doubtful if he could ever appear in public after all the propaganda and political support he has given the Vietnamese Communists against Cambodians." North Vietnam's strategy has worked so well that foreign analysts jokingly described General Lon Nol's powers as similar to those of a glorified "mayor of Phnom Penh." Now the Communists can exploit Cambodia's pervasive political and military weakness even more successfully in view of incurable difficulties in forming a viable, lasting cabinet under Lon Nol, who suffered a heart attack in February, was flown to Hawaii aboard an American air force jet for treatment, and returned in April, this time on a U.S. Navy propeller-driven DC-6.

"Nobody is loved by all the people," summarized Lon Nol's loyal "special assistant," his youngest brother, Lieutenant Colonel Lon Non, explaining away the rumors of discontent among senior officers allied with Sisowath Sirik Matak, the deputy prime minister to whom Lon Nol turned over power during his absence in Hawaii. "Even my brother is not loved by all," remarked Colonel Lon Non with a smile of broad-minded tolerance that scarcely concealed his own role in mustering much of the opposition to Sirik Matak and persuading Lon Nol to remain in power with a new cabinet. The result of the machinations of Lon Non and other influential politicians and officers was a state of semiparalysis, always fraught with the danger of a civil war within the greater war for national survival against the Vietnamese Communists. The real significance of the crisis was that it illustrated the fundamental ineptitude, lack of understanding, and weakness among national leaders far more accustomed to bickering and conniving among themselves than to battling the enemy. The North Vietnamese, in the meantime, found it much more expedient to watch the government disintegrate over political differences than to intimidate it into some semblance of unity by posing a direct threat against Phnom Penh.

The spirit of "la guerre populaire," as I observed it toward the end of March, seemed to indicate the malaise that afflicted Cambodia's intriguing politicians, generals and colonels. "We are glad to come and meet our people here," said Fernandez, now speaking Cambodian, as he arrived with his entourage at a village a few miles down the road from his camp. The general, who dared move through the countryside only in a military convoy, addressed a crowd of one hundred or so peasants gathered under a banyan tree in front of a monastery. The peasants, who had waited for six hours while soldiers forbade them to return to their homes and fields, listened impassively. Few of them bothered to smile, even politely. "La guerre populaire," as they had experienced it while Fernandez and his staff had been drinking and dining, had not been pleasant. The Viet Cong, apparently informed in advance of the army's plans, had attacked the village and monastery, which were guarded by two battalions for the official visitation.

Cambodian soldiers, far outnumbering the Communist attackers, had repelled them—for the moment. The bodies of two of the enemy—one a Vietnamese wearing "Ho Chi Minh sandals" made from a truck tire, the other a Cambodian—lay just beyond the bamboo fence surrounding the monastery. Curious Cambodian soldiers stared at them, but the villagers furtively walked by without looking. They paused and cringed, however, when several farmers arrived carrying two poles from which dangled bloodied slings made of multicolored cotton material used for women's sarongs. Inside the slings were the unconscious forms of two farmers, severely wounded by exploding shrapnel from artillery shells fired by Cambodian soldiers. Half a dozen student nurses, members of the propaganda team sent to the village for the day of "la guerre populaire," dressed the wounds and put the men in an ambulance for the bumpy ride to Kongpong Speu. The wife of one of the wounded insisted on sitting beside him. She was nursing an eight-month-old baby whose right arm bore the marks of a bruise suffered in a fall in a bunker during the shelling.

The specters of the wounded and the enemy dead outside the fence accounted in part for the numb reaction accorded Fernandez and his staff. Another reason, perhaps, was inbred suspicion of the general's pledges. "We will search for the enemy in the mountains and the forests," said Fernandez, talking into a microphone set up by the propaganda team. "We come not to destroy but to defend." Fernandez, a Catholic whose paternal grandfather had migrated from the Philippines to perform in the royal orchestra, attempted to play upon the Buddhist beliefs of the populace. "We come with monks from this monastery," he said. "We will protect the monastery chief. We will leave a colonel here with a battalion."

The general then introduced the chief of the monastery,

the Venerable Reth Sam An, who had sat behind him with three other orange-robed monks throughout the speech. The venerable, gaunt and bony-faced, still limping from a beating inflicted by Viet Cong troops, shouted anti-Communist denunciations. Fernandez and officers smiled among themselves when he suggested the army drive the Communists "as far as Hong Kong." Finally, the monk, who had fled the monastery for the relative safety of town several months earlier, led the crowd in a singsong prayer for peace. Dismissed, the villagers filed slowly, silently as before, outside the monastery. They did not carry the leaflets handed out by students and teachers. "We cannot read," a woman explained to a soldier.

If "la guerre populaire" was over for the people of the village, it was still in full swing for Fernandez and his officers. As soon as the peasantry had left, he invited us to another multicourse meal, accompanied by the usual libations. Boxes of canned tomato juice, supposedly for the villagers, held up the table boards. Bandages, always in short supply, served as napkins. The governor's Land Rover arrived with freshly roasted beef and chicken, still on the sticks on which his men had cooked them. Some monks looked on from a respectful distance, but otherwise none of the local inhabitants could watch, even from the monastery gates. The general and his staff were convulsed for most of the meal by a seemingly nonstop series of jokes. "I wish I could have had my wedding banquet without the wedding," was a particularly well-received sidesplitter that my interpreter translated for me.

The feast lasted nearly two hours, twice as long as the speech-making and propagandizing. Then, packed into their convoy of trucks, buses, Land Rovers, and jeeps, Fernandez, his colonels, and two companies of guards began the drive to town. Ahead of them, walking along the road, were the students, the low-echelon government workers, the teachers, some of them still carrying the leaflets they were supposed to have distributed among the peasants. Students and soldiers alike spoke disparagingly of the villagers, whom they looked on as social inferiors and suspected of collaborating with the enemy. "Don't trust the stars, don't trust the skies, don't trust in women, don't trust your mother who says she has no debt," said an army officer, quoting an ancient Khmer maxim, explaining why so many troops had to accompany his superiors on their trips to the field.

Judging from the attitude of Cambodian officers, however, one had to conclude the aphorism applied better to themselves than to the villagers whom they feared and despised. While General Fernandez, responsible militarily for all the provinces south of Phnom Penh to the Gulf of Thailand, was reveling amid "la guerre populaire," the Vietnamese Communists carefully prepared a series of ambushes on Route Four, the vital link from the capital to the coast. Several days later Communist soldiers, whom Cambodian and South Vietnamese troops had driven from the highway in a combined operation in January, fired on a convoy, destroying or damaging some fifteen vehicles. The battalion promised the village during Fernandez' visit was eventually withdrawn to answer a call for reinforcements.

"How can the villagers cooperate with the soldiers when they realize the Communists will come back as soon as they leave?" asked a teacher participating in "la guerre populaire." We already knew that local agents recruited by the North Vietnamese had visited most of the villages in the region. "They left behind their informers who will tell them everything about our visit," said the teacher, a self-assured French-speaking graduate of a lycée in Phnom Penh. The intimidating presence of informants among the populace illustrated the government's failure to penetrate, much less govern, the countryside. Since Sihanouk's overthrow, the Cambodian army had swollen from roughly 32,000 men to perhaps 180,000, but still was as helpless as it had ever been against a Vietnamese Communist force that probably never exceeded more than 10,000 regular troops actively engaged against Cambodians.

"When they started expanding in April of last year they had in mind an army of 500,000 men," said Fred Ladd, the political-military counselor of the American embassy since 1963, sent here in 1970 to coordinate the first shipments of American equipment since 1963, the year Sihanouk renounced all American aid. "They have learned that such an army is out of the question. They know every volunteer won't become a Sergeant York tomorrow. I guess they'll never go over 200,000." Ladd, a retired army colonel who once commanded all American special forces ("green berets") in Vietnam, nonetheless defended the Cambodian army in relative terms. "I don't think they even *had* a real army before 1970," he said. "Sihanouk ordered the soldiers to build roads or perform garrison duties. Now they're getting training and equipment."

Few observers, Cambodian or American, could dispute Ladd's contention that the army had certainly improved. Sihanouk, crowned as king by the French in 1941 at the age of eighteen, deliberately permitted the armed forces to stagnate after Cambodia gained independence, by diplomatic rather than military means, in 1953. He wanted a force strong enough to fend off encroachments against his power from within, but he feared the rise of a military elite that might ultimately overthrow him. His relationship with Lon Nol, defense minister in all his cabinets from 1956 to 1966, revealed his basic attitude toward the armed forces. On the one hand the prince (he abdicated in 1955 so he could participate more actively in politics) realized that he had to give Lon Nol enough power to suppress local leftists, who rebelled in 1966 in the rice-growing western province of Battambang. On the other hand, Sihanouk deliberately played Lon Nol against leftist politicians in order to hold the general's ambitions in check.

Lon Nol himself was as skillful in the game of Cambodian military politics as was Sihanouk. A conservative politically, he opposed Sihanouk's decision to rely on North Vietnam and other Communist countries for aid and friendship and addressed a series of reports to the prince in 1968 and 1969 on the dangers of Communist sanctuaries in Cambodian border regions. At the same time, the general, an enigmatic man of few words, sensed the futility of refusing to obey Sihanouk's orders. The prince was not only immensely popular—a "god-king" to the peasantry outside Phnom Penh—but had too many political allies in the capital. Not surprisingly, among Sihanouk's closest friends was General Fernandez, who, like most other Cambodian officers, had spent several years in training in France and emulated Sihanouk's own French-influenced social mannerisms.

As secretary of state for national security for the last three years of Sihanouk's rule, Fernandez was one of two or three principal figures in the movement of Chinese and Soviet arms and ammunition from southern Cambodian ports to Vietnamese Communist base areas and storage points. He had free access to the palace whenever he wanted it, and he was on close terms with Sihanouk's beautiful wife, Princess Monique, and her half-brother, Colonel Oum Manorine, secretary of state for national defense, with whom he coordinated details of the arms traffic. Oum Manorine was jailed for attempting a counter-coup, but Fernandez was totally absolved after the National Assembly voted him out of office two days before Sihanouk's overthrow.

"I was not for the Viet Cong," Fernandez shouted in an interview at his headquarters compound in Kompong Speu, explaining his renaissance from disgrace at the hands of the Assembly to command of an entire military region. "When I was in charge of national security I made reports in duplicate on Viet Cong activities. One was for Sihanouk and the other was for Lon Nol." For all these protestations, however, Fernandez seemed to typify the kind of artful compromiser who flattered the prince while appeasing opponents. The resurgence of Fernandez illustrated the desire among Cambodia's top leaders, particularly Lon Nol, to forgive and forget the former activities of those who claimed they were only following Sihanouk's orders in shipping arms or otherwise aiding the Communists. The majority of Cambodian officers, if not Lon Nol himself, did not object to Cambodia's de facto alliance with the Vietnamese Communists so long as the country remained stable politically and economically.

While literally all Cambodian officers today denounce Sihanouk and the Communists, the presence of Sihanoukists in the military structure has severely weakened its power. If some of Sihanouk's former cronies and allies are not exactly conspiring for his return from Peking, where he leads a government-in-exile, they still lack the will to offer much more than pro forma resistance to the enemy. Many of them, moreover, wallow in such hopeless corruption that no one knows precisely how many troops are now in the army. The sudden expansion of armed forces in the year after Sihanouk's fall provided the perfect opportunity for commanders to report the number of men in their units as far higher than they really were and to keep for themselves the payrolls of those who did not exist. This practice, common to all armies in Southeast Asia, might have gone unnoticed had American officials in Phnom Penh not demanded figures on real manpower strength so they could distribute weapons and other equipment.

"Cambodian authorities are investigating discrepancies," a senior American diplomat solemnly informed me. "They've sent special teams into the field to ascertain the size of each unit." For all these assurances, however, officers outside Phnom Penh said they had never heard of such an inquiry. The investigation, if it occurred, apparently was limited to rather cursory scrutiny of payroll lists in Phnom Penh. Far from eradicating corruption, it had the negative effect of arousing hostility among officers against Sirik Matak. "As long as Lon Nol survives there will be no difficulty," said General Fernandez, "but if he goes away, then there will be trouble." The general denied firmly that he opposed Sirik Matak but said "two or three" others were against him—a bold revelation in view of the government's claim of complete unity against the enemy.

The politics of Phnom Penh in some respects might resemble, as a young Frenchman who had lived here for several years remarked to me, that of "any small provincial town in France."

The comparison was doubtless apt, but the difference is that Cambodia's political and military difficulties may ultimately tip the balance in the contest for the Indochinese Peninsula. If the government cannot very quickly settle its internal feuds, in the opinion of worried American officials, then North Vietnam, always operating through local Cambodian "fronts" set up in Sihanouk's name, may permanently rule regions now beyond Phnom Penh's authority. Intelligence analysts in Saigon believe North Vietnam views complete restoration of infiltration routes and sanctuaries in these regions as prerequisite to defeating South Vietnam's army, at least as long as the United States supports the latter with aid and air strikes. The key to much of Hanoi's strength in South Vietnam before Sihanouk's fall lay, after all, in Cambodia's willingness not only to let the Communist countries ship arms for North Vietnamese troops through Cambodian ports but also to grant them sanctuary in vast border bases. The Vietnamese Communists, logically, did not resort to military means until diplomacy vis-à-vis the Cambodian government had failed them—in terms of long-range aims not in Cambodia but in South Vietnam.

Probably the most aggressively anti-Communist

Cambodian leader is Sirik Matak, who easily impressed Americans by seizing upon the concept of "la guerre populaire" and urging continued offensives against the enemy, particularly while Lon Nol was recuperating in Hawaii. Primary responsibility for conduct of the war, however, rested not with Sirik Matak but with a council of perhaps half a dozen generals in charge of a general headquarters within the ministry of defense.

The question, of course, is whether Cambodia's generals are at all better qualified militarily than Sirik Matak, by profession a diplomat who served as ambassador to China, Japan and the Philippines before Sihanouk temporarily "retired" him in 1968. Most senior Cambodian officers were trained by French officers in conventional infantry tactics that bear little relationship to the peculiar brand of hit-and-run warfare waged by Communist troops along all major roads leading toward Phnom Penh. Lon Nol himself, after having attended Saigon's fashionable Lycée Chasseloup-Laubat (ten years ahead of Sihanouk), began his career as a civilian magistrate under French colonial authorities in 1936. He did not enter military service until 1952, when he was appointed commander of Battambang province, and had no formal training until 1955, when he studied for several months at the French-advised Royal Khmer Military Academy.

Unlike Lon Nol, many of Cambodia's officers spent several years in France—or else, before 1963, studied in the United States under the old military assistance and advisory program. General Fernandez, for instance, has been to France three times: first in 1951 at infantry school, again in 1953 at staff school, and, finally, from 1959 to 1961 at the Advanced School of Warfare, the equivalent of the various war colleges in the United States for potential top officers. Often, however, the experience of training in France was more valued socially than professionally. Sihanouk himself was raised speaking French—and far preferred to discuss political and military problems in French than in Cambodian. (General Fernandez, like other one-time Sihanouk lieutenants, reflects his French background and close associations with the Prince. "Poof," he said, pursing his lips and turning up his palms in a typically French gesture of frustration, when asked if he knew whether or not any officers were still selling arms to the Communists.)

If an education in France was an asset in the milieu of Sihanoukist Cambodia, however, it proved almost useless when the fighting began in earnest a week or two after Sihanouk's demise. Cambodian troops were quite capable of dispersing peasant mobs shouting pro-Sihanouk slogans by firing into them, but they were almost powerless against Vietnamese Communist attacks on towns and villages along the frontiers. It was then, in April of 1970, that the army began commandeering multicolored commercial buses in which to rush what were known euphemistically as "mobile forces" in response to pleas for aid from besieged and beleaguered outposts on all sides of Phnom Penh. Untrained, ill-equipped and unwieldy, these units proved woefully incapable of defending all but the immediate environs of the capital, particularly since the Communists widened their campaign in pursuit of new base areas and supply routes after the cross-river incursions by Americans and South Vietnamese troops.

"Nobody dares say we support the new government or the old one," the wife of a village chief told me at the beginning of April, 1970, after a company of Communist troops had blared propaganda for several hours on behalf of Sihanouk's United National Front of Kampuchea, the ancient name for Cambodia. The woman, wearing traditional sarong and blouse, was standing beside her husband beneath the home on stilts where they lived with their eight children. Some fifty villagers gathered around as she recounted the incident in trembling tones. "The Viet Cong came into the village at eight o'clock last night," she explained. "They had a loudspeaker and shouted 'Long Live Prince Sihanouk' in Cambodian. They made us put up pictures of Sihanouk by the doors. They burned down the police station and the village office." The villagers, said the woman, "did not care about Sihanouk"—or, for that matter, Lon Nol. Their only concern was security.

Almost immediately, the government revealed it could not defend them against more raids and threats. A battalion of troops, packed into trucks and jeeps, roared by bewildered villagers the morning after the raid but did not pause en route to an embattled district town some fifteen miles to the north. The battalion was stymied near the village at a bridge blown up by sappers. Commanders deemed it too risky to go ahead by foot, or even to send patrols into surrounding countryside, studded with trees and stones behind which guerrillas could easily lie in ambush. A French-speaking major, in command of the convoy, explained that his troops, hefting Chinese, French, American and Russian weapons, were "well-equipped" but might run out of ammunition if the war expanded along the frontiers.

For all their equipment, the major's troops would have been powerless if the Vietnamese Communists had chosen to ambush the convoy, running almost bumper-to-bumper down the road. There was no artillery support and, at that stage in the widening war, no liaison with American or South Vietnamese airplanes. The major explained that his men had little time to worry about fine points of tactics or defense. The government was sending them from one trouble spot to another with no advance planning or even warning. "We have to defend all places at once," he said, before climbing into his jeep and leading the convoy back whence it came so his troops would be secure in their quarters before dusk.

The weakness of government forces in the spring of 1970 was understandable, but army officers could present no such excuses for the failure of a vaunted "counter-offensive" up Route Six, a critical highway north of Phnom Penh, the following September. For the first time in the war, according to Lieutenant Colonel Am Rong, the Cambodian army spokesman in Phnom Penh, Cambodian forces were "seizing the initiative" and beginning to drive the North Vietnamese from strongholds they had held since the previous spring and summer. Along with other reporters and photographers, I clambered into a Mercedes-Benz, the standard conveyance for reaching any of the fronts in this elusive, multifronted war, and hurried to the scene of the latest fighting, some sixty miles to the north.

The aim of the offensive was to open up Route Six as far as the town of Kompong Thom, a major government enclave some eighty miles north of the capital, but it was questionable if the special "task force" spearheading the drive could even get into the village of Taing Kauk, into which Communist troops had dug a complex network of trenches and bunkers. The weakness of the task force was all the more humiliating in view of the American role in the operation. Cambodia and the United States, after all, had solidified an unwritten agreement under which Washington was providing full air support (described as "interdiction of North Vietnamese supply routes" by Defense Secretary Melvin Laird) as well as new weapons, ammunition and even training for Cambodian troops in South Vietnam. Indeed, at least 1,000 of the 5,000 men poured into the offensive had just completed a three-week refresher course in South Vietnam after American transport planes had evacuated them from untenable positions in the sparsely populated, jungly northeastern provinces.

Two American planes, a slow-moving C-119 "gunship" laden with machine guns and a phantom jet on a photo-reconnaissance mission, were wheeling and diving overhead when I reached the tail of the task force near a blown-out bridge outside of Taing Kauk. Cambodian soldiers were lolling in hammocks slung between mud-spattered buses and French armored cars on which they had driven from Phnom Penh, and a work crew was attempting to rebuild the bridge with a new orange-colored steel girder, supplied by the Americans. I walked across the girder, past soldiers fishing and swimming in a canal by a rice paddy, to the "front," several hundred yards up the road. Bullets cracked and twanged, occasionally kicking up geysers of water in the rice paddies. French-trained junior officers shouted "Avancez!" Their charges, bunched together in defiance of commonsense rules of safety under fire, fought from trenches cut into the road by North Vietnamese saboteurs. A squad of Cambodians moved slowly toward the cement framework of an old schoolhouse. They poked through ashes and gaping holes in the walls, already bombarded by American planes. Automatic-rifle fire crackled from the shadows.

Major Hang Yieu, battalion commander, barked orders in Cambodian from one of the trenches. More soldiers inched forward along a wall beside the school-house. In a moment the rifle fire died down, and the American planes faded in the distance. Standing beside the major, I saw the bodies of three Cambodian soldiers lying next to an entrance to the schoolgrounds. "It is normal for an offensive," Hang Yieu remarked, somewhat laconically, neither sadly nor callously, as some of his soldiers stared at the bodies. Fifty feet ahead lay the bodies of two North Vietnamese, their hands still clutching a long pole on which had hung a sack of rice. Across from them was the body of one more Cambodian soldier, his white sneakers shining in the midday sun.

"It will be a long time before we reach Kompong Thom," said Hang Yieu as some of his troops fired a few final perfunctory shots into the school building, now apparently deserted by the last enemy snipers. As if to prove the major's point, most of his men slouched under some trees in the shade of abandoned village homes. Others foraged for pigs and chickens or drank water from a well. "We are waiting for our support," the major explained. A mile behind him, some of the "support" slowly lumbered forward—a few buses, armored cars, and hospital trucks identifiable by their red crosses. "We think maybe 2,000 or 3,000 Communist troops are ahead of us," Hang Yieu said, but his estimate seemed grossly exaggerated. Twenty or thirty snipers could easily have held up the entire column. The fighting on the fringes of Taing Kauk, in fact, dramatized the pattern of the operation, if not of the entire war. The enemy's main purpose was to harass, delay and pin down Cambodian forces while opening new supply and infiltration routes through eastern and central Cambodia to South Vietnam.

"Cambodian troops are advancing slowly but steadily," announced Colonel Am Rong (whose name, it has often been noted, seemed peculiarly appropriate) the morning after I returned to Phnom Penh. In fact, however, the North Vietnamese, sneaking around Cambodian positions, soon cut the road in several places behind them and threatened to surround them. It was all the Cambodians, supported by American air strikes, could do to fight their way into Taing Kauk, set up a more or less permanent base in the shelled, strafed, and bombed-out town, and hold the North Vietnamese at arm's length with occasional sporadic patrols into the tree lines. On my next visit to Taing Kauk, at the beginning of March, 1971, I discovered the commander of the task force, Colonel Um Savuth, stripped to the waist, sitting at a table in front of a Buddhist temple, guzzling glass after glass of American Black Label beer, purchased on the local "free market."

"I have not yet started to fight against the enemy base areas ahead of us. I am organizing local popular troops," explained Colonel Um Savuth, who Americans later assured me was "better drunk than most Cambodian officers sober." Colonel Um Savuth claimed he commanded some 12,000 Cambodian troops, but this figure seemed high to observers who had driven the twenty-mile stretch between Taing Kauk and Skoun, another bombed-out town at a junction on the way to Phnom Penh. Soldiers at small bunkered outposts along the road said they rarely, if ever, patrolled more than a mile or two in the daytime, and none of them had ventured more than a few hundred yards beyond the last guard post on the other side of Taing Kauk. Nor did it seem that Colonel Um Savuth had spent much time organizing popular forces, since most of the residents had fled the region. The ruins of Taing Kauk and Skoun were inhabited largely by families of the soldiers, who evidently believed they would remain where they were for quite some time.

If Colonel Um Savuth had failed to prove himself an aggressive commander, however, he had at least impressed upon his men one standing order: Behead any North Vietnamese soldier killed or captured in battle. "We never keep prisoners," explained one of the colonel's subordinates, also drinking beer outside the Buddhist temple. "After we have finished questioning a prisoner, we kill him." As a case in point, the officer said some of his men had interrogated a Vietnamese several days before my arrival and chopped his head off with a bayonet. At the forward post on the edge of town, one of the soldiers told me he personally delivered to Colonel Um Savuth the heads of North Vietnamese killed while attacking his position. Otherwise, said the soldier, "the spirit of the dead man could rise again in another body and attack us"—a belief that reflects the Buddhist backgrounds of most Cambodians and Vietnamese.

Soldiers admitted, however, they had relatively few opportunities even to attempt to carry out the colonel's special order. "A few nights ago a Viet Cong came on bicycle, got off, and crawled to our position," said one of the guards at Taing Kauk, describing a typical skirmish. "Our men fired, but he escaped. It was very dark at night. We did not go and search for him. We were afraid of the iron nails"—spikes implanted in front of the post for protection. In fact, the only Cambodian troops who impressed me as particularly aggressive or well-led were the Khmer Kampuchea Krom, Cambodians from the Mekong River Delta region of South Vietnam, trained into elite units by American special forces before Sihanouk's fall and sent across the border as units of the Cambodian army in the spring and summer of 1970. None of the "KKK," as they are generally known, were on the Route Six offensive, but I found them at other critical points defending the northern approaches to Phnom Penh against repeated attempts by the Communists to isolate the capital entirely from the countryside.

Some ten miles north of Phnom Penh, for instance, I met a wiry major named Kim Chi, born of Cambodian parents in South Vietnam's Vinh Binh province. Major Kim Chi, at forty-two a veteran of some twenty years in KKK units, had just led his battalion against North Vietnamese troops entrenched in a village named Kompong Popil, reached after a circuitous journey by sampan, motor scooter, military truck and, finally, foot. "I spread my soldiers on either side of the stream," said Major Kim Chi, walking across a bamboo suspension foot-bridge that bounced up and down like a spring beneath our steps. "Then I called in aircraft, but the planes couldn't see where to bomb and didn't drop anything. We went from house to house through the village driving the Viet Cong from their bunkers." Major Kim Chi's men also sank a camouflaged sampan in which the Communists had stored arms and food. "We are still finding rifles in the bunkers," he observed.

While Kim Chi was talking, some of the villagers tentatively peered from behind shuttered windows and half-closed doors. Most of them had fled, but those who remained seemed to welcome the presence of the KKK, at least in comparison with the Vietnamese who had occupied their village for the past few months. "Both North and South Vietnamese soldiers have been here," explained Yu Nguon, a gnarled shopkeeper who ground axes and knives for the village. "The North Vietnamese taxed us and stole our animals. They said we had to stay here and dig holes in case of bombing. The South Vietnamese also robbed us and violated women. Then the South Vietnamese left and the North Vietnamese came back and set up committees to rule us. We are glad Cambodian soldiers can now defend us." Yu Nguon sensed, however, the KKK would soon leave and fight elsewhere. "We need weapons and permanent protection," he said, realistically. "Otherwise we cannot live here. We must escape."

The KKK, totaling only ten or twelve battalions of several hundred men apiece, were most needed around the town of Kompong Cham, a provincial capital on the Mekong some forty-five miles northeast of Phnom Penh. "Every night we see trucks moving through the rubber plantations across the river," said a young KKK captain, Thuon Savan, in charge of an encampment ten miles upstream from Kompong Cham. "We called them by radio, and they said they were friendly troops, but they refused to give their unit number. We think they are North Vietnamese." Intelligence analysts confirmed that elements of three Communist divisions—the fifth, seventh and ninth—were based in the rubber plantations, periodically invaded by South Vietnamese troops attempting to protect the approaches to Kompong Cham and Phnom Penh. The KKK formed, in effect, the first indigenous Cambodian defense after the South Vietnamese. And KKK officers believed the North Vietnamese would cross the river in sampans and attack them as soon as the South Vietnamese had departed.

The question, then, was why the KKK were not capable of pursuing the North Vietnamese on their own—or at least of defending Kompong Cham and the road to Phnom Penh. The answer again seemed to lie partly in the form of leadership, in this case provided by Brigadier General In Tam, a career politician who, as president of the National Assembly, had helped to overthrow Sihanouk and then had assumed command of the entire region north of the capital. Like Colonel Am Rong, General In Tam explained that his troops were moving "slowly but surely" when asked why they spent agonizing hours, if not days, waiting for orders to advance down roads harassed only occasionally by enemy snipers. Several hundred North Vietnamese, dug into a series of villages south of Kompong Cham, blocked a brigade of In Tam's troops for a month despite American and South Vietnamese air strikes. Accompanied by a squad of In Tam's soldiers in an armored car, my interpreter and I drove eight miles down the road to the last outpost at a village named Rokor Koy. Villagers were just beginning to return to their homes—or what was left of them after allied bombing and shelling.

"We must finish building our camp," said the local commander, Major Ben Sawn, looking over fresh mounds of dirt and bamboo fences surrounding the outpost. "At least 200 of the enemy are only two kilometers away. If we advance too quickly, they will try to encircle us and attack us from our rear." The major's explanation may have seemed sensible, but he and his battalion were still at Rokor Koy when I visited him again three weeks later. "Now the Communists are spreading rumors. They're telling the villagers they intend to attack Kompong Cham again," said General In Tam. "The troops here won't advance again until we've built our defenses behind us. We're also waiting for all the villagers to return so we can defend them and they can help us." If nothing else, In Tam's remarks seemed to indicate how tenuous and fragile was the hold of his troops over the relatively small swath of territory that had supposedly been cleared, at untold cost of life and property, over the past two months.

Unlike other senior Cambodian officers whom I had met, however, In Tam impressed me as a personally sensitive man, alive to the suffering and fear of the people among whom he lived. He seemed to owe this sensitivity in part to a factor that may also have accounted for his military weakness: he was not essentially a soldier but a civilian administrator who had assumed rank and command for want of any other qualified officials. In my travels with him, In Tam displayed his political, if not military, expertise. "Don't drink so much," he said, smilingly, to a garrulous villager at a peasant wedding ceremony before handing him a 500-riel (approximately five-dollar) note as a gift. "Don't discourage your husbands and make them afraid," he remarked to the cringing wives of local village defensemen, whom we met at small outposts by the river. One of the men, wearing new military fatigues, clasped his hands together and bowed before In Tam in the manner of adoration and reverence reserved for political or religious, rather than military, figures.

In Tam's concern for his people was perhaps best displayed, however, at a meeting with commanders in his residence. "Don't let your soldiers steal chickens, don't kill animals," he warned. "Obey the good Buddhist doctrines. Your soldiers should be famous in war so the villagers will trust them." In Tam also advised the KKK not to set up their camps in villages. "People are afraid the enemy will shoot them when they shoot at the camp," he noted. "It's better to go far away to spare their houses." The commanders smiled knowingly to each other, then jumped in their jeeps to join their units. The KKK had advanced a mile or two to a stream, where they had killed one civilian (a farmer out fishing), whom they claimed to have mistaken for an enemy soldier.

If In Tam was not so harsh as career officers, he was as eager as any Cambodian for more and better American equipment. "I am requesting American rifles for all my soldiers," he said, standing near the new bunker complex in which he both sleeps and works. "If I have enough, then I will send my troops farther." All the KKK battalions carry American weapons, including M-16 rifles, with which they were supplied while in Vietnam, but many of the other soldiers still rely entirely on Chinese AK-47s and Soviet SKS semiautomatics or old American carbines. "It is very difficult obtaining enough ammunition and spare parts with so many different kinds of weapons," said In Tam, echoing one of the primary complaints of both Cambodian commanders and American officers sent here to expedite shipments of American arms. The United States has begun to compensate somewhat for this problem by equipping Cambodian battalions trained in Vietnam with M-16s, but Cambodian officials still said they needed much more than allotted under the present military aid program, which totals $185 million for this year alone.

"One of the problems is to get first-class weapons out of the hands of those on static defense around Government offices and into the hands of those who need them for fighting," said Fred Ladd, the American who probably knows the most about the Cambodian military establishment. "If you or I drive down the road we can find a battalion with as many as nine different kinds of weapons." Fairly soon, Ladd anticipated, the Cambodian military, armed entirely under Sihanouk with AK-47s, "would have to standardize toward both the M-16 and the AK-47." For the first time in the Indochinese conflict, in fact, the United States is supplying ammunition for a Communist-made weapon—AK-47 bullets, produced since September by a factory near Washington, D.C.

American officials recognize, however, the futility of even attempting to reform Cambodian units in the image of their American or even South Vietnamese counterparts.

"Anyone who talks about Cambodia in terms of American standards is immediately frustrated," said Ladd. "They wouldn't know what to do with all the equipment in an ordinary American brigade or battalion even if we gave it to them." Indeed, the most pressing need, according to specialists here, is to train the Cambodians to use the equipment they have. Americans are never really certain of the competence of Cambodian soldiers since the United States does not keep advisers with units in the field. Another problem, on a higher level, is that Cambodian commanders lack the managerial skills and experience needed to channel and coordinate the arrival and deployment of materiel throughout the country.

In the final analysis, if there is any reason for hope, it is the lingering spirit not of the army's Frenchified, stultified leaders but of the average soldiers, who seem either unaware or unfazed by the defeats and humiliations suffered by the army for more than a year. Shortly after Communist sapper attacks on the main airport at Phnom Penh and the oil refinery at the port of Kompong Som, formerly Sihanoukville, I drove to a typical bombed-out town named Saang, some twenty miles south of the capital on the Bassac, a main stream paralleling the Mekong. Vietnamese Communist and Cambodian troops had fought back and forth through Saang at least half a dozen times since last June. The Communists had last overrun the town toward the end of January, at the same time they attacked the airport. Cambodians recaptured Saang at the beginning of February and now were manning a bunker line beyond the last houses.

"My soldiers weren't well-trained at first," said Eang Nim, a craggy sergeant who had joined the Vichy French forces as a paratrooper in 1942. "We had time only to show the new recruits how to load their rifles and then sent them to fight after three days of training." Like most Cambodians, Eang Nim had never really expected a war. "The Viet Cong were our friends," he said. "They helped us clean our weapons sometimes when we met them. Then, after Sihanouk's fall, our government asked them to leave and they refused. They attacked and drove us back from the border." Eang Nim's soldiers insisted, however, the Viet Cong were now afraid of them. "Yesterday some VC saw our troops and ran away," said a young corporal in charge of firing a mortar. "We want the VC to fight so we can kill them."

Some of the soldiers pointed to a cluster of stones in a gully emptying into the Bassac. "The Viet Cong came ten meters from where we are," said a man in a bunker. "We fired at them before they could throw grenades at us. We found two of their bodies. You can still see the bloodstains." The soldiers claimed they didn't like their stationary positions and had asked to go on patrols. "Formerly the enemy looked for us," said a twenty-four-year-old corporal, Keo Sarath. "Now we should search for them. We should not stop here. If we have the chance, we will keep on fighting." Another Cambodian, Corporal Heng Ngan, was almost as critical of the South Vietnamese as he was of the Vietnamese Communists. "Both Vietnamese are alike," said Heng Ngan. "They have the same faces. The villagers are afraid of all Vietnamese. They want us to protect them."

The soldiers at Saang, looking toward a no-man's land of deserted houses and impassable roads, were evincing perhaps the oldest sentiment of Cambodia's traditional quarrel with the Vietnamese, bitter enemies for centuries before the arrival of the French colonialists more than a hundred years ago. In the absence of any real leadership, however, it was highly questionable whether or not even this kind of spirit, reflected among almost all the troops to whom I spoke, would really suffice. "We are not afraid, we are not afraid," the soldiers at Saang kept telling me, repeating a refrain, as if they were trying to convince themselves. "If the Americans give us enough arms, some new weapons and uniforms, we will win." While they were talking, literally on the last line of defense of the town, their battalion commander was returning from Phnom Penh in a Land Rover, followed by a platoon of his men in a convoy of three vehicles, laden with food and drink for his staff.

"We don't know anything about our government," said one of the soldiers, looking toward the commander's headquarters in a former schoolhouse in the center of town. "We only fight for our country."

chapter 8:

"Now the VC can go anywhere"

It was, as American officials were reluctantly recognizing, a Vietnamese war. One of the greatest mysteries of the changing war was how well the South Vietnamese would perform on their own, after years of American infantry, armored, and air support. You couldn't quite tell from the initial losses suffered by the ARVN in the 1972 offensive. The South Vietnamese often had their own way of regrouping and waiting it out—surviving without winning.

One place to go to try to assess the feelings of the South Vietnamese was a region under pressure, but still held by the ARVN. The Queson Valley, in a sense, offered a microcosmic view of the entire conflict as it had surged back and forth over the years. No other phase of the war could have better demonstrated the futility of a struggle that had really proven nothing except, possibly, man's cruelty toward man. No one will ever count how many thousands of Americans and Vietnamese died in the Queson, but it was the scene of some of the worst, underreported, fighting of the Indochinese conflict. American advisers, as they were leaving the valley for the last time, were no more sanguine about the prospects for real peace, much less victory, than was a youngish Vietnamese battalion commander with whom I went on a rather desultory patrol from an old American firebase named Ross.

The Americans, at least, were going home; the Vietnamese had to stay. Three months after I visited the Queson the North Vietnamese overran Ross and the nearby district town. A glib Vietnamese regimental commander, a colonel whom I had interviewed on the base, ordered a premature, needless retreat while reinforcements were already on the way in helicopters. The battalion commander, a major who had never shared his colonel's false optimism, nor his cowardice, was severely wounded— blinded in one eye. On my last visit to the region I heard the colonel had a comfortable desk job in Danang while the major was serving unhappily in regimental headquarters near Route One, pleading for another chance to rejoin his men in the field.

Queson Valley: May, 1972

It has been a long war for the American adviser on Landing Zone Ross, a patch of dirt and cement large enough for a dozen 105- and 155-millimeter cannon and a couple of companies of infantry. He returned here eight months ago and found the war had come almost full circle from the time of his first tour with the same South Vietnamese regiment, in the same valley, in 1965 and 1966.

"Oh, things were a little different," says the adviser, a lieutenant colonel whose main job, now as then, is to call in American air strikes for the South Vietnamese. "It was very dangerous to drive up the road, and the ARVN didn't patrol much in the valley." Just about the time the adviser was going home from his first tour, the American marines were settling in here. LZ Ross, says the adviser, a West Pointer with silvering hair, was named for a marine colonel. You still see the names of marines painted on some of the big boulders near the top of the base, where the commander of the fifth regiment of the second ARVN division keeps his command post.

Then the marines pulled out of much of the Queson—pleasant rolling farmland sinking into forbidding, jungly hills on either side—and troops from the army's old Americal division began sweeping the valley. The soldiers also left their imprint on Ross, half a mile or so up a rutted road from the market town of Queson, itself some twenty miles from the lowland highway leading to Danang, fifty miles up the coast. Black peace signs, considerably more popular among army soldiers than marines, are splashed on some of the rocks. The initials "FTA," for "Fuck the Army," appear on one boulder just below the newly painted symbol of the fifth regiment, a medallion showing three mountain peaks over a dragon emerging from the sea with the slogan, "Vuon len," "rise up, overcome."

The Americal, for all the recalcitrance of some of its soldiers, may have fought harder and longer for the Queson than the marines. The names of the old Americal firebases, scraped off lonely hilltops, still dot the situation map in the little sandbagged briefing room in the fifth regiment headquarters. There they are, red and black grease-pencil marks on the grid lines, sobriquets imbedded in the memory of the GIs who defended them but otherwise largely forgotten: "Kala," "Irene," "Mimosa," "Melon," "Judy," "Grant," "O'Connor," "Pleasantville," "Marge," "Mary Ann," "Mildred," "Young," "Barrier," "Center." Among them perhaps only Mary Ann achieved much fame. Before dawn on March 28th of last year, North Vietnamese sappers pierced its flimsy defenses, overrunning most of the base and killing thirty-three GIs—the highest number of American dead in a single ground attack in the history of the second Indochinese war.

If the Americans never defeated the North Vietnamese, they at least drove most of them out of the valley. "We opened the road in the middle of 1968," says a Vietnamese officer in the town of Queson, a district center still bustling with betel-chewing women selling rice and meat in open stalls in the central market and crafty shopkeepers peddling cloth and hardware to farmers from outlying hamlets. In fact, before the last Americal soldiers went home several months ago, it was safe to drive eight miles farther up the valley to another smaller district center named Hiep Duc, on the other side of a steep, rock-strewn slope known as "Lion Hill" to the Americans, or "Hon Chieu" to the Vietnamese. Among the hills beyond Hiep Duc, in jungle sparsely populated even in moments of peace, American soldiers until the end could expect to encounter regular North Vietnamese troops lodged in almost impenetrable caves and cement-lined bunkers bound by tunnels and trenches.

In the populated regions of the valley, however, security was such that South Vietnamese troops did not immediately replace the Americans after their withdrawal. It was not until early April, several days after a new North Vietnamese division, the 711th, had launched a series of attacks around Hiep Duc, that the fifth regiment was rushed in a convoy from the southern lowlands, reopened Landing Zone Ross, and reoccupied a string of old hilltop firebases and outposts. "Now the VC can go anywhere. We don't have enough troops," says Major Nguyen Thai Buu, sitting on one of the new sandbag piles thrown up on Ross a few weeks ago. "My soldiers are very tired," the major goes on. "They have been walking every day for the past six weeks. We have to keep the VC away from Queson. If the fifth regiment leaves Ross, they will go all the way to the lowlands."

As it is, says Buu, who has fought at one time or another

among almost all the hills and valleys in the Queson region since graduating from military academy at Dalat seven years ago, the ARVN have abandoned the valley beyond Hon Chieu, rising three miles to our west. "We began fighting around Hiep Duc on April 11th," says Buu, commander of the fifth regiment's fourth battalion. "We left there on April 14th to keep the VC from moving closer to Ross." Major Buu, who rose with the regiment from platoon leader to company commander to battalion executive officer before his appointment as battalion commander a year ago, does not appear humiliated or even slightly embarrassed by the retreat. "We attacked the VC at Hiep Duc for three days," he says. "They attacked us for one day. We killed fifty-one of them and captured sixteen weapons."

It might be rather unfair, in fact, to interpret the withdrawal of Major Buu's battalion as a defeat in itself or even as an adverse reflection on its performance. It was just that the 711th division included two fresh regiments, besides an old one bloodied by the Americans, and South Vietnamese commanders rightly anticipated the possibility of the sudden loss of the entire valley. At the same time, two provinces to the south, in Binh Dinh, North Vietnamese troops plunged all the way to the lowlands, driving the South Vietnamese from a series of small towns and villages and cutting Route One, the main north-south highway. Three provinces to the north, the enemy had poured across the demilitarized zone, driven the ARVN from a string of firebases once held by the U.S. marines and army soldiers and were on their way to surrounding the provincial capital of Quang Tri, finally overrun at the beginning of May after the collapse of the third division.

Nor was Hiep Duc immediately abandoned after Major Buu's retreat. "As our battalion moved back," says Buu, a slender broad-chested son of a small landowner from Quang Ngai, "the VC surrounded Hiep Duc and attacked the regional force troops left inside the town every day and every night for several days." Finally, the district chief, responsible for both the civilian populace and local territorial troops, ordered the town's evacuation and de facto surrender. "On the way from Hiep Duc to Queson, the RF lost an entire company," says Buu, "and the district chief himself was killed." For Major Buu, accustomed to roaming the hills and lowlands ever since he was a small boy riding his father's water buffalo, the flight from Hiep Duc was the beginning of a series of tactical withdrawals, none of them necessarily defeats as such, all of them characterized by heavy losses on both sides.

"We had to move back to keep the VC from moving to the east," says Buu. "As we moved back, we attacked them three times. One time we contacted two battalions and requested air strikes but they arrived too late. A day later we searched the area and found twenty bodies of VC. Everywhere we go, the VC mortar our battalion." The VC (a term Major Buu uses indiscriminately to include both Viet Cong guerrillas from South Vietnam and regular North Vietnamese troops) by May had overrun a couple of old American firebases and are still lodged on one of them. "Air strikes hit the top of one hill and the side but missed the enemy bunkers," says Buu. "When our battalion moved close to the fire base, the enemy shelled it with mortars. They don't care about their own casualties."

Major Buu talks easily, softly in the final glow of daylight. Looking over the valley, he sounds almost academic as he tries to explain why the North Vietnamese seem more determined than his own soldiers, why his battalion has had to retreat time and again just to keep from falling apart and to protect Ross and the rest of the valley. At the age of thirty-two, younger than average for a battalion commander, he does not seem to have lost confidence or faith in his army. There is, one gathers, a rational explanation for almost everything, ranging from the defeat at Quang Tri to the corruption of some, if not most, of the country's leaders. Major Buu's long bony fingers, his jut jaw, and a scar around his left eye all seem to give him the appearance of an experienced jungle fighter, a commander who would be an asset to any army, and yet he is a man marked prematurely by a curious sense of resignation.

Major Buu has just returned from a patrol some four miles west across the valley from Ross. "Almost every day we have some contact with the enemy," he says. "Today we find three of them and kill one. The other two run away." Somewhat deprecatingly, he unfurls a newly sewn National Liberation Front flag, green and red with a yellow star in the middle, found in the pack of the dead soldier, and offers me an NLF medal showing a pith-helmeted guerrilla hurling a grenade at a tank with the initials "US" on it. "The enemy now uses the tactics of close contact," says Buu. "They set up strong points: two men with AK-47 rifles and one with a B-40 rocket launcher. With these they can hold a company or a battalion for a couple of days. We have to destroy the strong points in order to get through the area." One question Major Buu asks is whether it is wiser to request air and artillery strikes, often inaccurate, or to risk high casualties among his own men by storming enemy concentrations on the ground.

"We don't want to fight like the VC," says Major Buu, who attributes the scar around his eye to a childhood rock fight, but has twice been wounded in earlier campaigns. "We try to save our men. Any time we have close contact, we call in air and artillery." Sometimes, however, highly disciplined enemy troops respond by fighting harder rather than falling back. "The VC are very smart," says Buu. "When they see tac air, they just move forward toward our men. Now they are determined to hold their strong points. They stay until death, and it is very difficult for us to recapture any place once it falls into their hands." Buu also notes the adverse effect of air power on the South Vietnamese. "If you do not depend on it, you fight better," he says. "If you depend too much on air power and artillery, you know you just do nothing. In the end, in battle, you cannot depend on anyone. You have to fight for yourself."

Buu admits, however, that without American airpower the enemy would probably have overrun Ross and Queson in the first few weeks of the offensive. "At the present, air power holds the enemy," he says, shrugging. "We don't want to lose our men. Perhaps we save them for the long run." That afternoon, while he was on patrol with half his battalion, American jets and helicopter gunships were blasting away as usual at the sides of Hon Chieu with 500-pound bombs and rockets. "Outstanding!" shouted the regimental commander, Colonel Nguyen Huu Luu, when the commander of the third battalion, holding the top of Hon Chieu, reported by radio that half a dozen enemy soldiers had died within fifty feet of his bunkers. "The Communists will be killed, all of them," Colonel Luu announced to his American adviser, calling in the strikes, but his triumphant smile vanished as the battalion commander radioed that he and several of his men had just been wounded by enemy mortar fire.

"The NVA are attacking right now," Luu rasped. "We need more gunships." His adviser patiently called in more strikes while a Vietnamese medevac chopper whirled in to pick up the casualties. "For the last three days Ross has received 82-mortar fire and 75-recoilless rifle fire," said Colonel Luu, in a lull in the fighting for Hon Chieu, overrun two days before by the NVA and recaptured the next day by the ARVN. "The reason they shell us—they do not want our artillery to support our troops in the field." If the enemy overruns and holds Hon Chieu, said Luu, who spent eighteen years with the first division somewhat to the north before coming to the fifth regiment a year and a half ago, "they can fire at us more easily from better positions."

Luu appears to have resolved not to yield any more territory—for tactical or any other reasons. "We must hold what we have," he says that evening over dinner with his officers in a tent behind his command bunker. "We must fight to the last man." That night the North Vietnamese renew their attack on Hon Chieu. Colonel Luu, in white shorts and T-shirt, again shouts at the American adviser for more air support. "Please keep one gunship on station all night," he demands. The next morning he is even more impatient to wipe out the enemy mortars, apparently firing from abandoned rice paddies around the base of Hon Chieu. "We must know exactly where they are," he admonishes an intelligence officer, who has been pointing rather vaguely at tiny black dots on the situation map.

As soon as the briefing is over the colonel orders Major Buu to patrol the road and rice paddies around Hon Chieu in search of the mortarmen, probably no more than a squad. A few hundred yards from Ross, in a tin-roofed village named Son Lanh, nine armored personnel carriers and a couple of tanks line up in front of soda stands that once peddled PX Cokes in cans to GIs. A company of Major Buu's infantry, 110 men of his battalion of 320, lounge by the road or haunt the food stalls, purchasing tea and pork rinds, fish and vegetables for their day in the field. It is an hour later, almost nine, before the infantry, followed by the armored, is ready to push through a crowd of curious children toward the barbed-wire village gate, opened by a gap-toothed old man wearing faded, threadbare olive-green fatigues and rubber sandals.

While the APCs and tanks flounder through a rice paddy that is just yielding a new crop, the infantry vanish into the trees in front of us. Major Buu, riding on an APC bristling with antennae that link him both to Ross and to his own officers on the ground, stands up and yells at stragglers to spread apart. Passing the cement opening of an enemy bunker, our column slows down and forms an arc in front of a dark, silent tree line. "We are going slowly because this area is very dangerous," Buu explains, as more of his men disappear into the trees. "On our left are many more bunkers and tunnels. We must search around here very carefully." A minute later, after the infantry has finished checking the tree line, the column again begins to rumble, this time across overgrown fields probably not farmed for several years. Some of the soldiers on Major Buu's APC yell and point. We are passing under a tree laden with ripe pineapplelike fruit. The APC stops while the soldiers knock them down with their rifle butts.

It is almost lunch time. While the infantry checks another tree line, Major Buu orders the armored to halt. A couple of soldiers produce blackened pots from their packs and boil water on a small fire at the base of a tree that provides just enough shade to shield us from the noonday sun. One of the soldiers passes out little soup dishes, chipped and cracked chinaware with blue-enameled designs on them, filled with rice. Another offers meat soup, which we pour over the rice, and glasses of hot tea. While eating, Major Buu keeps talking on the radio. "We've intercepted a VC message," he says. "They are planning to shoot B-40 rockets at our APCs. Some of our soldiers have seen the VC in front of us. They are hiding under camouflage, perhaps a company of them." Buu orders a couple of APCs to "recon by fire"—spray the bushes with their machine guns—and calls in artillery from Ross.

"We will wait for the artillery," he says, as shells from Ross whistle overhead, slamming into the brush a few hundred yards away. "It is difficult to attack the VC in their underground tunnels and bunkers." One of the tanks begins firing with its big single gun, igniting a small blaze in the dry grass. A lieutenant on our APC listens for a moment to a call on the radio. "Now the VC are moving to another area, toward the hills," he reports. Again, Major Buu orders the infantry and armored to resume their advance across the paddies and scrub. "When the VC shoot, the distance is very close," says Buu, accounting for why his soldiers have not been fired on. "Maybe ten or fifteen meters." We stop again, this time shielded from view by overhanging branches, near the foundation of an old house blasted away in some bygone campaign.

Some of the soldiers in front of us are chattering excitedly. Three old women, chewing betel nuts, wearing conical hats, followed by two little girls and a small boy, emerge slowly from behind the bushes. Soldiers hover over them while Buu questions the boy—not impatiently, but in matter-of-fact, carefully monotonous tones. The boy looks more nervous than scared, as if he were reciting a lesson for a teacher but not quite giving the right answers. After a minute or so Buu turns to me with a somewhat cynical grin. "Yesterday they see a company of VC with 82-mortar," says Buu. "This afternoon the VC have a squad here, but they run away when we fire the artillery and they don't see where they run." There is no way of telling, really, how much the villagers know. "They always say, 'no see, no hear,'" says Buu. "Now we have to search this village carefully." Buu orders his soldiers to poke into half a dozen or so thatched-roof huts, invisible among the trees—all that remain of the hamlet.

While the soldiers are searching, Buu again discusses enemy tactics. "Whenever they go away, they leave men to attack our flank, to observe and control our activities," he explains. "But if they decide to attack us, they never run. At the present time, we operate very slowly and carefully because we have to defend our rear, because we don't know where the VC are." Again Buu reflects on the limitations of artillery and air strikes. "It is hard to judge them effectively," he says. "If we are firing on only one strong point, no sweat, but if they have two or three or four, it is very difficult. While we are firing on one, the others will fire on us. They support each other." Buu also notes the contrast between rear-echelon training and battlefield realities. "When we study," he says, "we keep one platoon in the front, one in the rear.

But here we send in three-to-five-man groups. If they have no contact, a platoon or company follows them to search the area."

The enemy, having decided this time not to fight, has totally eluded Buu's men. After checking by radio with two of his company commanders, Buu orders the column to turn around. Several soldiers prod the women and children, who get up and begin walking with the infantry. "We will question them further at headquarters," says Buu. The APCs are thundering back through the empty fields when an explosion kicks up a cloud of dust and smoke a quarter of a mile to our left. It is the parting shot of the 82-mortar squad, a blast that reminds our nine APCs, two tanks, and 110 men of our failure to find them. The APCs stop while a soldier on one of them fires in the general direction of the impacts with a 50-caliber machine gun. "We don't know where they are," says Buu. "No sweat," he grins, and orders the column to keep rolling.

It is 5 p.m. of a sleepy, sun-splashed afternoon, the end of an eight-hour day, as our patrol clanks to a final halt on the dusty road in the middle of Son Lanh village. Old women display bottles of beer and soda, and soldiers hastily drink them down or wash themselves with water from the village well. Major Buu and two or three of his officers settle into a little shop and purchase Bah Muoi Bah "thirty-three" beer poured solicitously by a young girl into large ice-filled glasses. "The regional forces are setting up an ambush and they will return to the village by sundown," says Major Buu. "When it is dark, the VC may come back," he admits. "We will stay on Ross at night to defend the perimeter."

In a war characterized by more watching and waiting than real fighting, it has been a fairly typical day. After seven years of it, Major Buu exudes neither optimism nor much disillusionment. "There are bad people in government. You only find all good people in heaven," he says. He offers three reasons for the collapse of the third division in Quang Tri.

First, it faced superior forces—approximately three divisions. Second, it was a new division, staffed with the worst officers from other units. And then, he says, with just a trace of bitterness, "The United States is not eager to help South Vietnam." Otherwise, why would the Americans have waited until after the offensive began to offer the latest M-48 tanks and other new equipment to the ARVN?

"They knew the North would invade South Vietnam," he says, "but they do nothing until afterward. It was the same way when they gave us good weapons in 1968 after the Tet offensive." Buu's remarks on American aid epitomize the response of a broad range of South Vietnamese officers and civilian officials, convinced that Washington has somehow sold them short again. Yet Buu does not think his army will completely fall apart. "American withdrawal is not too much of a problem," he says. "We have enough manpower and capability. All we need are the arms and the airpower." Nor does he think the 711th division can threaten the Queson Valley forever. "They are only waging a campaign," he says. "If we can stand it for two or three more years without defeat, they will go away. The difficulty is the government must use its troops to protect an entire territory while the enemy can hit a certain place and run. Sometimes it looks as if they are everywhere. We must follow a policy of flexible endurance."

The question, then, is what motivates the major to keep enduring, if not always fighting. "I do it for my living, my family, my country," says Buu, who is paid 24,000 piastres (sixty dollars) a month to support his wife and two little girls in Quang Ngai. "My country is the most important," Buu insists, as we walk back up the road from the village to the base. "I do not agree that most Vietnamese fight only for their families." It is difficult to say whether religion might also be a factor in his outlook on the war. "I believe deep in my heart in Buddhism," he says, but so do some of Saigon's most outspoken antigovernment politicians, who favor compromise and reconciliation with the enemy. Unlike many of his soldiers, Buu disdains the wearing of a Buddhist good-luck charm around his neck: "It brings neither good nor bad luck."

Buu's loyalty to the army, if not the Saigon government, probably lies imbedded in early childhood indoctrination by his petit bourgeois family, including stories of Viet Minh persecution of his merchant uncles. "My family was against the policies of the Viet Minh because we owned our own land," says Buu, raised in Duc Pho district, thirty-five miles south of the provincial capital of Quang Ngai and eighty miles south of the Queson. "The Viet Minh jailed those who they thought were too rich or were landlords. They accused them of corruption and killed or executed them. They were very cruel." Buu's father died of natural causes in 1952, but the Viet Minh the next year picked up an uncle in Duc Pho and tried him in public. "They said he was guilty of using the blood and sweat of the people, and they imprisoned him for two years," says Buu. "Then he died."

Buu denies that his family owned much land ("just a couple of hectares"), but in a class war he inevitably identifies by birth and upbringing with the elite. Sent through primary and high school in Quang Ngai, he then studied in Saigon for a year before sitting for the entrance examination for the military academy at Dalat. His younger brother now studies law in Saigon, while his three brothers-in-law are all junior officers, one in the air force, two in the army. It might never be possible to fathom the family and communal relationships responsible for Buu's early rise to a battalion command, but it seems probable he has certain influential friends and relatives. "I believe in President Thieu," he says. "I don't believe in any party but the army. We don't like to fight, but it is our responsibility to fight against the Communists to the last blood." It is not surprising, in view of such sentiments, that Buu speaks with contempt of General Duong Van "Big" Minh, who is associated politically with peace-minded Buddhists in Saigon, and dismisses negotiations in Paris as a "waste of time."

The sun is again setting over the Queson, and Major Buu gets up to check the outer defenses of Landing Zone Ross, criticized by the Americans as too thin on barbed wire and sandbags. One of the advisers radios an American gunship—a twin-tailed C-119 known as "Stinger"—to fire on an "enemy concentration" on a hilltop to the west. Colonel Luu enthusiastically suggests a combined "American-Vietnamese marine invasion of North Vietnam" and then discusses the merits of "napalm" versus "powdered tear gas" in "denying areas to the enemy." The adviser, patient as always, explains that napalm "breaks apart and burns out vegetation" while tear gas powder just "settles in and stirs up when you walk through it." Colonel Luu has decided the simplest way to get the mortarmen around Hon Chieu may be to "defoliate all the ground around it."

The next morning, after the briefing, Major Buu gives me the names and address of his wife and mother in Quang Ngai. The American adviser warns me the road from Queson to the lowlands isn't as secure as it once was; I drive down the valley in a jeep with a young lieutenant on his way to see his father-in-law. Regional force troops are walking slowly along the potholed macadam with mine detectors. and a couple of charred trucks lie in a ditch where they were tossed by explosions a couple of weeks before. In the next district south of the Queson, North Vietnamese forces already have penetrated as far as the abandoned north-south railroad, paralleling Route One along the coast. It is still reasonably safe, however, to drive down Route One to Quang Ngai, a town of small shops and old homes now crowded with refugees from nearby districts terrorized of late by local guerrillas. Major Buu's wife, a schoolteacher, lives in a sturdy two-story cement building crowded with relatives, half of them, it seems, below the age of ten.

A tiny woman, expecting her third child in several months, Madame Buu has not seen her husband since the offensive began in early April. Even before that, he rarely was home more than one night a month. "He is a soldier. He must be far away, for many days and years," she says. "Two years ago he was wounded in the leg and had to spend a year at home. Since then, the longest we've been together is a few days during Tet." Madame Buu, eight years younger than her husband, married him five years ago at the age of nineteen. She opens an album of photographs showing her and her husband strolling by a lake at Dalat, attending a party of officers, sitting in a garden. They both had gone to the same schools in Quang Ngai. Their families had known each other for years. Above her, on a whitewashed wall, hang tinted photographs of Buu's parents, his father looking somberly through large-rimmed glasses.

"He chose the military life when he was very young," she says. "He will continue as long as the war lasts. He will be a soldier forever." A friend translates the lines beneath his picture in the 1965 military academy yearbook. "I grew up in war, I was a farmer, a cowman," they say. "I chose the military life because my country suffers. I want to see my country at peace and happy again." Major Buu's mother, considerably heavier now than when she posed for the photograph on the wall, says she prays for peace, prays that her son will return, prays the war will end, in fact, "in two more months." She is not counting, however, on any immediate answer to her prayers. Beneath a table are packages full of belongings hustled from relatives' homes in Duc Pho before the road south of Quang Ngai was cut in mid-April. A next-door neighbor is filling sandbags outside.

"I am afraid the Communists will return and put many people in prison," the elder Madame Buu says. "Then we must go to Saigon or Danang, to a place that is free of Communists." Buu's wife, holding one of her little girls, also prays for peace but seems more hopeful. "I always think my husband will defeat the VC," she says. "Then he will come back in a few more weeks or a month. The war will end and peace will come to Vietnam and the world, and the American and Vietnamese soldiers will not die any more. The VC will not occupy Quang Ngai. The soldiers of South Vietnam will not be defeated. President Thieu will bring peace to Vietnam."

Her mother-in-law, perhaps recalling the Viet Minh era of the early 1950s, smiles indulgently from across the room.

chapter 9:

"Just observers"

After the peace came the peace-keepers. One could never tell what the Poles, Hungarians, and Indonesians really thought about it all, but the Canadians did not hesitate to talk to anyone who asked. For them it was great getting a Vietnam tour on their records, but then it all turned sour as the peace degenerated and they realized they were accomplishing little or nothing. The presence of the Canadians was refreshing, however, because they spoke so frankly. (The few remaining American officers, many of them members of the Four-Party Joint Military Commission, set up for sixty days under the intricate terms of the Paris agreement, were forbidden to talk to reporters at all. In any case they were embittered by the way the press had covered the war and were hardly prone to speak frankly even when coaxed into background or off-the-record briefings.)

The sense of futility among Canadians was beginning to

set in when I visited some of them at a town named Phan Thiet on the coast some six weeks after they had gotten there. They were still hopeful, but they chafed under restrictions and obstructions. They did not think their government would want Canada to remain on the peace-keeping team much longer. Within another six weeks Canada decided to withdraw the entire contingent at the end of July, rounding off exactly six months of interesting if wearisome, largely useless, service.

It seemed ironic that I personally had my most dangerous experience in Vietnam two weeks after the cease-fire. It was all the more ironic that the violators, in my case, were not the North Vietnamese, whom the Canadians blamed for most of their problems, but South Vietnamese pilots. The experience of direct exposure to air strikes did give me some idea, in a small way, of what the war had been like for millions of others caught unwittingly in the midst of indiscriminate bombing. You can talk endlessly to survivors and victims, but you can never imagine it until you've lived it.

Binh Phu: February, 1973

A row of thatched-roof hootches strung along a rice paddy here seems to mark the shadow borderline between the so-called "liberated zone" of the Viet Cong's Provisional Revolutionary Government and the territory controlled by the national police and army of the South Vietnamese Government in Saigon. From the nervous, almost frightened expressions on the faces of the old men and women crowded into their homes at the close of a sun-splashed, seemingly placid morning, you sense you are walking in a limbo between two sides. They cast inquisitive, not unfriendly glances at a couple of foreign reporters as we walk by them after a stroll through rice paddies and bush quite firmly held by young Viet Cong soldiers carrying Chinese AK-47 rifles and American M-16s.

One old man shakes his head when I point across the rice paddy toward a Viet Cong flag fluttering from the end of a bamboo pole near a single hootch. He shakes his head just as emphatically when I point down the row of rice paddies toward a cluster of tree-shaded homes flying the flags of the South Vietnamese government. None of the hootches on this particular dike between paddies fly any flags at all—in clear contradiction to the "rules" of the new Vietnamese war in which flag-flying is required as a minimal symbol of loyalty to one side or another.

"VC, VC," a couple of kids inform us, gesturing toward the hootch near the VC flag. "No VC," they say as they wave down the dike on which we are standing. It is not necessary to let us know the presence of the VC across the rice paddy, however, for we have just been guided on a tour of the area by one Le Minh Hoang, an eighteen-year-old Viet Cong soldier who slung an AK over his shoulder and led us across the paddies. He was seemingly oblivious to the presence of South Vietnamese armored personnel carriers on Route Four only a mile or so away—well within range of their fifty-caliber machine guns.

In fact, we were partly responsible for the apprehension of the peasants around us since a spotter plane and helicopter had both swung low over the paddies while we were with some Viet Cong soldiers in a hootch. Since South Vietnamese police on the road through the village had tried to keep us from entering the "liberated zone," we concluded that the spotter and the helicopter were dispatched in part just to see what we were doing. Shortly after the spotter and helicopter had buzzed away, South Vietnamese artillery opened from near the road. Our AK-hefting guide seemed unfazed as the rounds whistled overhead and landed amid some bushes a few hundred yards ahead of us. It was the same kind of show of government force a stream of other newsmen in the same area had witnessed over the past few days. For Le Minh Hoang, however, the sound of the artillery seemed a matter of small concern. "No," he said, grinning, as the two correspondents crouched beside an old burial monument near the trees. Hoang seemed to know from the sound that the rounds were well overhead.

Government soldiers did not appear to have seriously attempted to dislodge the Viet Cong from portions of this village beyond the main road. "Bombing," said Hoang, as we passed a couple of hootches blasted away by artillery or bombs, but most of the buildings remained intact—and there was no sign of any attempt by government soldiers to move across ground through the rice paddies. "Welcome peace, welcome agreement," said the Vietnamese lettering in the hootch where we met Hoang and two other soldiers at the beginning of our guided tour. Copies of the newspaper *Ap Bac,* named for the village near Saigon where Viet Cong forces scored a major victory nearly a decade ago, were pinned on the wall.

"Peace is coming. Everybody can do their daily work in the rice paddy," Communist cadre told the people of Binh Phu. "The National Liberation Front will not harm anyone in the village. The war has ended." As if to underline this point, women and children crowded around us as we entered the hootch where we met Hoang and another rifle-bearing soldier, Nguyen Minh Hung, who scrawled his name and his age, nineteen, in my notebook.

If the "liberated zone" of this divided village some sixty miles southwest of Saigon is beyond the military power of the Saigon regime, it is almost deceptively easy for a civilian to go there. After slipping down a tiny path off Route Four, the main road through the Mekong River delta, one walks along narrow footpaths across a network of tiny canals. Although government flags flew from all the buildings near the road, we had no compunctions about informing the local citizenry of our desire to get to the portion of the village controlled by the National Liberation Front. We just drew tiny pictures of the NLF flag—two stripes with a star in the middle—on the palms of our hands, and villagers smilingly pointed us in the right direction. Our main concern was to avoid the South Vietnamese police, whom we had left behind on the road after indicating we were returning to Saigon. They did not attempt to follow us after noting our empty car by the road—largely because they could not be sure of their own security. The attitude of the villagers on both sides of the conflict seemed to indicate their underlying desire for "peace" as opposed to clear-cut support for one side or the other.

A couple of old women in a sampan offered us a lift down a tiny canal to a clearing where an old man in a pith helmet pointed at a couple of Viet Cong flags and then at the bombed-out remains of what once was a large thatched-roof home. He delegated two small boys to lead us deeper into the "liberated zone" after we indicated we wanted to meet some Viet Cong with rifles. The soldiers themselves emerged from nowhere after we arrived at their hootch. They volunteered to pose for photographs as if they were actors in a set-piece scene. Grinning, they pulled little Viet Cong flags from their pockets, raised them on bamboo poles and adjusted their rifles in classic guerrilla poses.

More soldiers emerged from a much larger wooden structure another mile or so across the paddies. Among them were civilians, old men as well as women. Amid the whine of occasional artillery shells, they pointed to bunkers and gestured down another path leading us back to government-held territory. One of the Viet Cong asked us for cigarettes and warned us against the government police back on the road. As we walked down the path, the soldiers vanished back into the shadows. It was not until we were alone on the dike, walking back, that we noticed the absence of men and women in the paddy—and the scared looks of those who seemed to fall on neither side of the invisible line between opposing forces.

The struggle for Binh Phu illustrates the delicate nature

of the Vietnam "truce" signed in Paris on January 27. Although the Viet Cong still control much of this village, peasants report that South Vietnamese soldiers have driven the VC from many hamlets nearer the main road over the past few days. "They tore down VC flags and put up their own," says a teen-aged boy in the central market after we return to the road. "Two days ago the Viet Cong were almost on the road." Despite a post-cease-fire offensive, however Saigon soldiers clearly lack the strength, in terms of manpower or local support, to annihilate the Viet Cong. At one village, shopkeepers report that residents of a Viet Cong hamlet freely come and go on shopping expeditions every morning from eight to ten. "No one stops them," says a woman selling cakes beside the road, "but the police discourage them later in the morning." While we are talking, two national policemen with radios appear to take us by jeep to the district headquarters two miles to the east. The efforts of Saigon officials to discourage contact with the VC technically violate the provision of the agreement permitting free movement between "zones" under government and Communist control.

Artillery and small arms fire represent much more serious violations of the agreement, but members of the International Commission for Control and Supervision of the cease-fire remain optimistic about instilling some measure of real peace and security to the region. "It's a challenge," says Colonel Robert Screaton, commanding the Canadian members of the team at the nearby center of Mytho. "I'm not frustrated yet." Screaton admits, however, that he and other team members are powerless to act on their own. "It's up to the Four-Party Joint Military Commission to decide who controls what ground," he says. "We're here to help them do what we hope they want to do."

It seems unlikely that the JMC—composed of representatives of the United States, North and South Vietnam and the Viet Cong's provisional revolutionary government—will function with much if any equanimity.

For many of the villagers on Route Four between Binh Pho village and Mytho, it is already too late. "The Communists raised their flags so the government soldiers shell into my hamlet," explains a young high school student named Le Van Lam. "They've been shelling since the day the cease-fire was signed." While we are talking on a path beside the rice paddy, a girl screams uncontrollably. Two other women beside her are sobbing. "The soldiers grabbed my mother as she ran away from the hamlet," screams the girl, named Nguyen Thi Lahn. "They made her pull up one of the flags. A grenade wired to the flag exploded and killed her."

The fighting reflects the cynicism of both sides in the war as they attempt to claim as much territory as they can before the ICCS finally delineates areas held by one side or the other. "The VC came into the hamlet, dug bunkers and raised their flag the night before the cease-fire," says Lahn. "They said peace would come at eight on Sunday morning, and then they left." While we are talking, three more VC flags appear over the trees. The South Vietnamese troops, under fire from VC soldiers up and down the treeline, are powerless to drive them out.

"Please intervene with the field commanders to stop the shooting," an old woman urges me, in the belief that I am a member of the ICCS. Vietnamese air force skyraiders and F-5 "freedom fighters" dive down on the tree line. The explosions send shockwaves over the rice paddies. Across the road, South Vietnamese troops fan out toward another tree line over which hang several more VC flags. "My home is destroyed. Ten people in my hamlet have been killed," says an old woman. "Peace, peace, they promised us peace. We had everything we needed—cows, pigs, food. Now they're all gone."

Phan Thiet: March, 1973

The young Canadian staff officer for once was excited. "Get in my jeep," he offered. "I'm going out a little way. I want to find out what's happening." With some embarrassment, as we were driving on a dirt road inland from this coastal fishing town, the officer explained that his investigation was entirely unauthorized. That is, his own commander on the Canadian delegation of the International Commission for Control and Supervision knew where he was, but representatives of the other countries on the ICCS had not endorsed the expedition and would doubtless have frowned on it had they been aware of what he was doing.

We bounced down the road for two or three miles while the major, a Czech-born, British-educated career officer named John Hasek, quickly sketched the scene. "They've been fighting for a hamlet named Ap Tan Binh two kilometers away," he explained. "It's abandoned, blown away, but the people still come out from here to work the fields. The ARVN are well established where we're going. They send out patrols at night to Ap Tan Binh. And the PRG [the Viet Cong's Provisional Revolutionary Government] also come in at night. That's where the clashes occur."

It was an almost classic example of low-level confrontation in Vietnam, but it was the prospect of peace-keeping rather than fighting that seemed to have aroused Major Hasek's interest. "Both sides are requesting an investigation through the Joint Military Commission," said the major, a veteran of the peace-keeping force on Cyprus. "We're hoping the JMC will ask the ICCS to carry out its own investigation. It would be the first real chance we've had since coming here. So I just want to get out here and take a look before all the ICCS people begin falling all over each other."

The momentary enthusiasm of Major Hasek epitomized that of most of the 250 or so members of the Canadian delegation of the ICCS. Highly trained, with previous experience on any of a dozen other Canadian peace-keeping teams from Kashimir to New Guinea to Yemen, they came to Vietnam after the signing of the truce on January 27th exuding much the same verve and camaraderie as American combat officers in the early years of the war. Strolling along the streets of Saigon in their dark green bermuda shorts and green berets, they were novelties in the jaded eyes of taxi drivers and bar girls lamenting the loss of the American GIs. (The berets, in fact, were not new at all. They were made, it was soon revealed, by the same Canadian manufacturer that turned out headgear for the American army's special forces, known popularly as "the green berets.") Specifically ordered to explain their role to anyone who asked, the Canadians did not hesitate to pause for a chat or a lengthy interview on street corners, on the terrace of the Continental Hotel, in the dark recesses of tattered GI bars or anywhere else they happened to lurk in their few off-duty hours.

"The point about the mission," a major from Calgary explained to me when I accosted him on the steps of the Continental, "is that its supervisory capability lies in the terms of the agreement." Technically, he said, the Canadians and the other members of the ICCS—from Hungary, Indonesia and Poland—weren't peace-keepers at all, "just observers." In contrast to real peace-keepers, who were armed on Cyprus to shoot to kill if necessary to keep order, the ICCS representatives in the field could only carry sidearms for self-defense in case of extreme emergency. "At no time will we become involved in armed conflict," said the Canadian, who had served six months in the Suez in 1967. "We report infractions if requested by the Joint Military Commission. We observe, but we have no power to change a situation." For all these limitations, however, the Canadians were determinedly optimistic. "We think the cease-fire will eventually come," said the major, who was awaiting orders to go to one of seven regional ICCS headquarters at critical points from Hue and Danang in the northern provinces to Cantho in the Mekong River delta. "We're ready to go in the bush, all of us," he added with a kind of gung-ho aggressiveness. "We know what we're going to do."

It was two months afterward, in late March, that I drove some one hundred miles east of Saigon to visit the regional headquarters at Phan Thiet and encountered Major Hasek in his jeep outside the old American military advisory compound, now used by the Joint Military Commission. Wiry, athletic, tough-looking, Major Hasek kept himself trim by running two or three miles each afternoon around the small airbase beyond a cemetery on the edge of town where the ICCS maintained its regional offices. He was friendly with the local South Vietnamese officials and the Americans at the new Area Resettlement and Reconstruction Office, the successor to the old Civil Operations for Revolutionary Development Support team operated by the departing U.S. Military Assistance Command Vietnam. He and his ICCS colleagues lived in a small hotel near the market and dined quite often at either of two pleasant, leisurely Chinese restaurants tucked into a row of shops and coffee stands. It was not, if you thought about it, a bad way to spend a hardship tour. It was clear, however, that Major Hasek was not only extremely bored but damned impatient for action.

"Now, if an investigation gets launched, both sides are going to try to get possession of the village," he noted with the terseness of a field commander reviewing his latest situation reports. At the outpost nearest the abandoned village a South Vietnamese officer saluted Major Hasek as he climbed out of the jeep and explained what was happening. The major wanted to venture closer to the village, but the South Vietnamese dissuaded him. "There's no security out there," Hasek agreed, "and anyway I'm not supposed to be here at all. There'd be hell to pay if anything happened to me. I'm supposed to be back at the ICCS headquarters twiddling my thumbs and looking at reports." The South Vietnamese, of course, were just as much to blame for the lack of security in the village as were the Viet Cong. "They've been throwing in mortar rounds and artillery all morning," said the major. "No idea where they're landing. We're liable to get hit if we go out there without ARVN troops. They think the PRG are massing to attack."

It was one of the lesser ironies of the skirmish that it actually worsened as a result of the immediate possibility of an investigation. Both the South Vietnamese and PRG members of the Joint Military Commission, which also included American and North Vietnamese representatives for the first sixty days after the signing of the truce, had indicated they would ask the ICCS to look into the matter, but for entirely different reasons. The PRG was protesting incessant artillery and air strikes by the ARVN while the RVN (Republic of Vietnam) charged the PRG with ambushing a patrol early one morning near an old French fort built in the Viet Minh era. The battle was petty, in the overall context of the fighting even after the cease-fire, but Major Hasek relished it as an excuse to get out of town and possibly to launch the first ICCS investigation requested by both sides in the war.

The great irony of the skirmish, however, was the sheer inability of the ICCS to do anything about it even though it was happening within binocular range of the ICCS regional compound, perched on a gently rising bluff overlooking the lowland plains as far as a range of blue green hills in the haze some twenty miles to the west. "It's our resident battle," Major Hasek remarked somewhat wearily as we turned back from our venture into the field and drove up to the compound. "It's kind of like the oldest established permanent floating crap game." Laconically, he handed me the binoculars through which I could see a South Vietnamese L-19 spotter plane turning lazy circles over dusty rice paddies. Shells occasionally boomed in the distance, smoke gusted where they hit, and the sounds of the explosions reverberated seconds later. "That way every day," said Hasek, before changing for his afternoon run around the base. "The RVN have combed all over there.

We've seen a dozen air strikes at least. It's a real Mexican standoff."

But what was to keep the ICCS from initiating its own investigation before receiving self-interested requests from members of the Joint Military Commission? Nothing, technically. In fact, however, the leaders of each of the ICCS delegations here seemed to while away much of their time in endless debates inside a shack built by GIs several years ago and remodeled as the ICCS meeting room. The pattern of debate was fairly typical. "We have no difficulty getting the other members of the commission to report unfavorably on RVN violations," Ambassador Michel Gauvin, the chief Canadian delegate to the ICCS, observed, "but we can never get the Poles and Hungarians to agree on a negative report concerning the PRG." Indeed, Canadian regional team leaders had difficulty just persuading the Poles and Hungarians that the roads were safe enough for them to travel.

"That's not the first problem," said the leader of the Canadian regional delegation, Colonel Frank Campbell, standing beside Major Hasek and me as we gazed at our "resident battle" through the binoculars. "The two most responsible parties, the South Vietnamese and the PRG, both have to guarantee security or the Poles and Hungarians won't go anywhere." Colonel Campbell, tall, graying, cautious, rule-bound, did not quite share Major Hasek's impetuous desire to at least get to the fighting without the approval of the other regional delegations. Rather, as the officer in charge of half a dozen Canadians based here, he preferred to engage in gentle persuasion, careful review of the terms of the agreement, and exposition of the facts. Still, for all his patience, he could not help but reflect the exasperation of the entire Canadian contingent in Vietnam. "My feeling is we must get into a much more active observer role," he suggested. "We shouldn't be waiting for complaints. We should just pile into our jeeps and make our presence known. There's nothing in the Paris agreement to keep us from initiating our own investigation if all four members approve."

As it was, however, the colonel was not entirely unhappy with the record of investigations in the first sixty days since the signing of the agreement. He noted with real pride that the ICCS at Phan Thiet had just produced one of the first unanimous reports in all Vietnam on quite a serious incident, in which six persons were killed and thirteen wounded by a mortar round fired into the central market of Phan Thiet. Yet his description of the investigation did more to illustrate the basic weakness of the ICCS than to prove its long-range potential. "First thing we did when we got the complaint from the South Vietnamese late one evening, we agreed we would get a copy to the Joint Military Commission first thing in the morning," said the colonel. "We argued we must put on a time limit for the JMC to reply or the PRG would delay the investigation, but it still took another day for them to say anything. Then the PRG refused to support the investigation." At this point the Canadian delegation might have abandoned the quest, but the Poles and Hungarians for once could not plead that the road to the scene was insecure. "We were in luck because it happened right in town," said Major Hasek. "It gave us a chance for a test case. The Poles and Hungarians had to go along. The mortar landed only a few blocks from where we live."

The Poles and Hungarians had yet another excuse, however, for delaying the investigation. The leader of the Indonesian delegation, rotating that week as chairman of the regional center here, could not reach the ICCS chairman in Saigon by telephone to request his formal approval. "You can't go anywhere these days without written authorization from Saigon," said Campbell. "Three days later we finally got approval from the Hungarian ambassador, who was serving that week as ICCS chairman." Was it just by chance that the line to the Hungarian chairman was perpetually out of order? Or was the Hungarian, as Canadian ICCS members argued, deliberately attempting to sabotage an investigation that might reflect badly on the PRG? For that matter, why did a regional ICCS need the approval of the ICCS in Saigon at all? The agreement does not require any such time-consuming bureaucratic procedure, and Canadian officers strongly opposed it while blaming the Poles and Hungarians for conjuring such a wasteful regulation. By the time the investigation was really launched, five days after the mortar round was fired, much of the evidence of the blast had disappeared.

All the delays probably had little substantive effect, however, for the most the Poles and Hungarians would have conceded under any circumstances was that a mortar round had indeed been fired. The Canadians were still happy because enough people happened to have been standing around the marketplace to verify conclusively that the round had landed and exploded, and the Poles and Hungarians had no choice but to sign a report alleging just that much. The happiest observers of the entire proceeding, though, were the PRG and North Vietnamese members of the Joint Military Commission, whose own regional delegations were confined to barbed-wire compounds across the airstrip from the ICCS. The report, after all, stated that the investigating team "could not conclude that a cease-fire violation had occurred," a blanket vindication of the Viet Cong guerrillas who had almost certainly fired the round.

"So we may say that the ICCS had a very objective opinion and has come to a very right and reasonable conclusion," said a North Vietnamese major, Phan Huynh, whom I met in the conference room of his compound shortly before the departure for Hanoi of all the North Vietnamese JMC delegates at the end of the sixty-day post-cease-fire period. "So maybe the shell exploded by itself. We think nobody fired it," reasoned Major Huynh, smiling pleasantly, offering me banana candy and pouring from a bottle with Russian lettering on it a glass of vodka distilled in Hanoi. His tone hardened and his smile tightened into a glare, however, as he accused the United States and South Vietnam of conspiring to frame the PRG. "I want to know for what purpose the US and RVN delegations on the JMC have fabricated the circumstances of such an incident," he asked, looking at me quite sternly beneath a portrait of Ho Chi Minh and a large North Vietnamese flag, yellow star on red field, hanging on the otherwise bare wall. "It is correct to say they have brought up such an incident in order to hide their own violations," he rasped. "While they launched many 'nipping operations' against the liberated zones, they also trumpet about what they have done in order to gain the sympathy of the people, in order to say the truth belongs to them."

The North Vietnamese were so pleased with the verdict of the ICCS in the mortar case that the leader of the delegation sent a formal letter thanking the commission for its "thorough, impartial investigation," a gesture that did more to diminish rather than increase the Canadians' satisfaction. "Sure," admitted Colonel Campbell, showing me a copy of the North Vietnamese letter, "the investigation proved nothing in itself." As a next faltering step, however, he hoped to induce the Poles and Hungarians to cooperate on real investigations into incidents of a much more serious nature. It was a sign of the fundamental lack of rapport between the delegations that the Canadians rarely met with the Poles and Hungarians outside the conference room even though they lived in the same hotels in town and occupied offices within fifty feet of each other on the air base. The Canadians were often more successful in dealing with the Indonesians, an indication of the common attitude of both delegations toward the entire peace-keeping mission. The Indonesians, reflecting the anti-Communist policy of their government, tended to follow the lead of the Canadians while opposing the Poles and Hungarians.

Not surprisingly, a conversation with the head of the Polish delegation at Phan Thiet left me with a sense of bafflement and disappointment. I first saw Colonel Marian Kozlowski in the former American military advisory compound watching a Steve McQueen movie about auto racing. Officers from the other ICCS delegations were also there, banded together in their own national cliques, clearly identifiable by their uniforms among the American civilian officials and contractors. Like the Canadians, Colonel Kozlowski was personally courteous when I buttonholed him after the movie, but entirely uninformative on the subject of the mortar incident. "It is an honor to perform this duty despite the heavy task," said Colonel Kozlowski, speaking to me through a bright young civilian interpreter who the Canadians were convinced was an intelligence or political agent—and possibly the real leader of the Polish team. But why did the investigation take so long to begin? "Perhaps Saigon is too full of complaints," he replied blandly, "and besides there is trouble with the telephone." Why didn't the ICCS investigate the real fighting outside of town rather than piddle away its time on a stray mortar round? "We are prepared for all kinds of incidents," said the colonel, an air force officer trained as a navigator on Soviet-built transportation planes. "If the JMC asks us, we will do it."

But the JMC never asked. Whenever the PRG wanted an investigation, the South Vietnamese opposed it. When the South Vietnamese wanted an investigation, the PRG opposed. The only question that mattered for either side was who controlled what territory. If PRG forces were in the village and the South Vietnamese were shelling, then naturally the PRG welcomed the prospect of ICCS inquiry. If South Vietnamese troops were patrolling territory in their hands and Viet Cong guerrillas ambushed them, the South Vietnamese righteously demanded the aid of objective observers, that is, if South Vietnamese troops still held the territory after the ambush. There was also the secondary question of which specific phase of Phan Thiet's "resident battle" really mattered to which side. Talking to members of the PRG delegation in a cement-block building by the airstrip beside that of the North Vietnamese, I couldn't be quite certain we were referring to the same places. A PRG liaison officer conceded, however, that "RVN forces now occupy one strategic hamlet," presumably near the outpost to which Major Hasek and I had driven the previous day. The PRG, of course, held the rest of the area, even though "the people were forced to leave by the RVN."

Finally Major Hasek had to concede defeat—or, more properly, another frustration. "Doesn't look as if anything will come of it," he told me, as we sat drinking cups of thick black coffee in a snack stand across the road from the JMC conference room, a white clapboard building once used as an American army chapel. "They're still talking over procedure." The major sank back psychologically into the lethargy of the assignment. But "we're not giving up," he said, in the pursed-lip style of a field officer stubbornly clinging to a position that he knew was untenable. The sense of depression, of futility, among Canadian officers at Phan Thiet was typical of the weary bitterness of Canadian officials at all levels. In the Mekong River delta region, a strong-minded young diplomat named Manfred Von Nostitz, in charge of the Canadian delegation at Cantho, denounced the unanimous ICCS reports as "meaningless" and said the Canadians and Indonesians would submit separate reports fixing the blame when necessary on the PRG or the North Vietnamese. "There's no cease-fire," he told me not long after my visit to Phan Thiet. "The North Vietnamese are rolling across the Cambodian border. There are four North Vietnamese regiments in Chuong Thien province south of here. Three of them arrived since the signing of the cease-fire."

At Cantho, Canadian officers serving under Von

Nostitz, who was one of the few civilians leading a regional delegation, claimed the Poles and Hungarians had delayed communications with Saigon by fiddling with the radio equipment. They said the Poles and Hungarians, if induced to visit the scene of a cease-fire "violation," would listen respectfully to statements implicating the Viet Cong and then deny having heard them on returning to headquarters. In one case, the killing of fifteen persons by a grenade thrown into a Buddhist pagoda, the Canadians and Indonesians finally signed their own independent report after the Poles and Hungarians discounted the word of a monk that Viet Cong agents had threatened to blow up the pagoda several days beforehand. "We were told by our briefers that it has been estimated that there have been some 7,000 incidents since the cease-fire came into effect," said the Canadian secretary of state for external affairs, Mitchell Sharp, after a swing through Indochina in March. "Out of these have emerged only thirty-one requests for investigations by the ICCS. . . . From these requests just two Commission reports have emerged," one of them presumably on the mortaring in Phan Thiet.

The Canadians, notably Sharp, had been skeptical about the efficacy of the ICCS from the time that American diplomats had pressured them to participate before the signing of the truce. As evidence, they could cite the unpleasant precedent of the original International Control Commission, formed under the 1954 Geneva agreement on Indochina with delegations from Canada, Poland, and India. "Bitter, frustrating experience with the ICC. . . . conditioned the Government's wary approach to any new involvement in Vietnam," said an official Canadian press release, explaining why Canada originally limited its membership in the new ICCS to an initial trial period of sixty days. Sharp lengthened the trial period until the end of June after his March visit, but his skepticism turned into outrage with the shooting down on April 7th of an Air

America helicopter flying nine persons, including one Canadian captain, one Indonesian officer, two Hungarian officers, and two PRG liaison officials, over PRG territory to an ICCS team site near the Laotian frontier. "The general situation has not improved; in fact it has deteriorated," said Sharp in a speech to the Canadian House of Commons. "If it does not improve very substantially, it will be clear that by continuing to serve in the ICCS, we would be staying on to observe not a peace, not a cease-fire, but a continuing war."

It was just that, a continuing war, that Major Hasek could glimpse every day through his binoculars from the ICCS regional center by the airstrip at Phan Thiet. "Last Saturday an ARVN patrol got ambushed in the area of an old abandoned French fort," he remarked. "Obviously, they'd been doing the same thing with the Viet Minh twenty years ago. There's an old American firebase out there too, Firebase Sherry. They've been fighting this time for the past six weeks. It just goes back and forth." The sense of history somehow forced a pause in our conversation. The pattern of a generation of warfare would not change, and Major Hasek knew it. "We're actors in a charade," said one of the Canadians. "There's nothing we can do but watch while the real war goes on all around us. That's what makes it so hard."

Along Route Thirteen: February, 1973

It is the middle of a lazy Sunday afternoon, and my driver and I are sitting on bamboo benches in a small hut beside the road talking to a young North Vietnamese army lieutenant. The conversation is dragging somewhat because we are awaiting the arrival of the colonel who commands all the Communist troops on a five-mile stretch between the towns of Lai Khe and Chon Thanh, some forty miles north of Saigon. "Big guns shoot here," says the lieutenant, named Tran Kim, and we all turn and look dutifully at a cloud billowing on the horizon two or three miles away.

In any case I am not overly impressed. Obviously the North Vietnamese are putting on a slight propaganda show for us. I have driven up from Saigon to see how far the road is open in the new era of "peace" in Vietnam, and I would rather find out what's really happening than accept the honeyed words of a skilled Communist political officer. I drove this road for the first time on April 6, 1972, several days after three divisions of North Vietnamese troops poured across the border from Cambodia, knifed south through the flatlands and the rubber plantations, and surrounded the provincial capital of An Loc, ten miles north of Chon Thanh, fifty miles north of Saigon. It is the old rubber road, built first by the French to move the rubber from the plantations to Saigon, then rebuilt by U.S. army engineers before they finally withdrew in 1970.

It is a dull black ribbon through the tinder-dry yellowing bush. It is the kind of road you would never remember, never care to drive again, unless you had to, for business or for war. I drove up the road many times in April and May of 1972, always thinking the South Vietnamese would punch through to An Loc, but they were always stopped by small-arms fire, rockets, and ambushes at a critical point by the shelled fragments of an old watch tower several miles north of Chon Thanh. Now Chon Thanh itself is surrounded, and the South Vietnamese have abandoned the struggle to reopen the road. They have left it to the North Vietnamese, the remnants of three divisions scattered and scarred but never defeated by incessant American air strikes that ended only on the day the cease-fire was actually signed in Paris, January 27, 1973.

It is several months since I last drove up Route Thirteen, past a dirt road bypassing the South Vietnamese base at Lai Khe, then back on the main highway. We (my driver and I) have left our car at the last South Vietnamese outpost, two or three miles north of the base. South Vietnamese guarding the outpost only stared idly as we parked the big 1950s-era Chevy by some rolls of concertina wire stretched across the road. A couple of miles ahead of us, shimmering in the sun, looking deceptively near, we could see a white banner strung across the blacktop. The South Vietnamese guards did not object as we picked our way through the wire and began walking up the highway. There is, after all, a cease-fire. The Paris agreement specifically states that anyone can move freely from one zone to another. Although the fighting has raged along Route Thirteen for months, we are relaxed, unconcerned. It is a new era in the Indochinese conflict.

"Hoa Binh Roi Kong Canh Nha," reads the first line of the sign, actually white letters on a red field rather than entirely white, as we thought when we first saw it from the South Vietnamese outpost. "Hoa Hop Toc Chung Huong Hoa Binh," says the second line. "Peace now, don't fight, national reconciliation, and enjoy peace," is the English translation. Beside the sign are two flags of the Viet Cong's Provisional Revolutionary Government, red and blue stripes with gold stars in the middle. A North Vietnamese soldier, looking almost as weary as the South Vietnamese down the road, has idly waved us over to the bamboo hut. He is twenty-one, and he comes from a town near Hanoi— my driver quickly gleans these details. But the soldier, wearing green shirt and black trousers, says he cannot really talk to us until his superiors have arrived.

Lieutenant Tram Kim, when he appears a few minutes later, announces that he is "the chief of the gate" and has been fighting around here for two years. He carries a Chinese pistol on his American army belt, a pair of sunglasses in the pocket of his green shirt and two American- or Japanese-made pens. "Every day, they bomb and rocket this area," says the lieutenant, as my driver interprets for me, but it is hard to imagine any real bombing on this particular afternoon. I keep asking questions, and he orders the soldier who first met us to cross the road and find the commander, who, he assures me, can tell us "everything."

"The Saigon soldiers can come here to talk, too," says the lieutenant, smiling pleasantly, talking in Vietnamese to my driver, who serves as an interpreter. "But they must leave their weapons behind." As if to underline the propaganda mission of the men at the gate, he looks up at the leaflets and calendars with photographs of Ho Chi Minh that are hanging from the thatched ceiling. It is so hot and I am getting so bored with this conversation that I am beginning to fall asleep when we hear the crump of a bomb a mile or so away. It is so commonplace, this sound of exploding bombs, that none of us even turns to look, though it does vaguely occur to me that these bombs are not "friendly" any more or, if they are still friendly, that I am definitely in unfriendly territory.

This idle thought evaporates as the colonel, the top commander, finally emerges from the bush accompanied by a young soldier who speaks English. "I studied the language for three years in Hanoi," explains the soldier, named Do The Vinh. "I was a cargo surveyor in Haiphong harbor." It is a matter of more than passing interest to me that Vinh admits he is from North Vietnam since Hanoi officially refuses to concede the presence of any of its soldiers in South Vietnam. Only true southerners, native-born guerrillas fighting for the National Liberation Front, have risen up against the Saigon regime and the American imperialists, if one is to believe the propaganda. I am still more excited, however, by the prospect of a long discussion on "life on the other side," and I am vaguely wondering how to open the interview when we hear the thud of more explosions a mile or so away.

"Don't fear—far away," says Vinh, and we get on with the interview. "The commander's name is Truong Minh Sanh," Vinh writes carefully in my notebook (the whole sentence, not just the name). I am about to begin the interview with the colonel when a rocket lands one hundred feet or so beyond us. It is fired from a spotter plane still some distance away, perhaps as much as half a mile, circling lazily, almost invisible against the bright rays of the sun. All of us turn and look toward the nearest shelter, a typical bamboo-lined fighting hole, but Vinh, the colonel, and I keep talking. It is hard to analyze why. Either we are difficult to scare or all of us—the North Vietnamese, my driver and I—fail to comprehend the danger. "I do every work, as the commander tells me," says Vinh when I ask him rather off-handedly how he's been whiling the time away since coming south three years ago. The commander, who looks somewhat like the driver, only thinner, smiles ingratiatingly and hands me a letter to deliver in Lai Khe.

A somewhat odd request, I am thinking, but I smile back and accept the letter, a handwritten appeal to South Vietnamese officers and soldiers to "cease shelling and bombing in our liberated areas," to "exchange letters when necessary," and to "visit our side without weapons." The first bomb targeted for us lands a couple hundred feet away as I am putting the letter in my pocket. Hastily I scribble my last notes—that the colonel is wearing an unlikely outfit of green shirt, blue fatigue pants, and black Ho Chi Minh sandals—as he and the rest of us spring up and wait just a moment in indecision.

Then the colonel and the lieutenant jump into the nearest fighting hole. Another runs across the road. Vinh waves for me to follow, but my driver shouts for us to begin walking back to the car. Neither of us wants to get caught on the North Vietnamese side in a battle. Besides, we cannot quite believe the bombing will go on since the South Vietnamese at the last outpost know we are here. We are on the road, walking under the banner, when we hear the distant jet scream of the next bombing run. At the graceful long whistle of a 500-pound bomb we hit the ditch by the shoulder, then are up and running a second after it explodes in a cloud of black and gray smoke fifty feet or so away. We cannot run back to the North Vietnamese fighting holes because we do not know where they are any more. We must keep on the road or the pilots will see our movements in the bush, assume we are enemy troops, and kill us with their miniguns.

We hit it again at the sound of the next whistle, again across the road, but we know we cannot run for two miles. We walk and hit, walk and hit with each scream of the jets. We must get away, away from the North Vietnamese outpost. I am hoping the South Vietnamese know we are civilians (my driver's shirt is white and mine is yellow), but pilots of jet aircraft cannot always make such distinctions. And even if they could, they could probably not sight the bombs with such accuracy as to land on the North Vietnamese positions while avoiding the two people walking away from them. I am sure the pilots have mistaken us for the North Vietnamese when one of the bombs lands one hundred feet ahead of us on our side of the road. We do not have the shoulder to protect us this time, and the dirt and shrapnel spout up in a black geyser, flying by us, over us. We are unhurt and force ourselves to get up and walk—toward the spot where the bomb would have killed us had we been there just seconds before.

It is the moment between strikes when the fear claws at you, and you wonder why you are here and if you will get out alive and you are sure you will not but you have to keep moving. The fear mounts as you hit the dirt and crests into a sense of calm at just that instant when you are flat in the brush and you hear the long crescendo of the bomb and you wonder if you will get up again or if you will get it on Route Thirteen the way thousands of others got it when you were covering the campaign from April through June.

You think dimly, subconsciously, for the duration of a fleeting image, perhaps, of the others whom you knew who died on Route Thirteen. There was Lieutenant Colonel Burr

Willey, a soft-talking southerner who was advising a South Vietnamese regiment at Chon Thanh when you first met him in his sandbagged bunker in May. It was just as hot then as it is now, and Colonel Willey was fretting because the Vietnamese, as always, were refusing to move swiftly against just a handful of North Vietnamese troops dug into old bunkers near the road. "It's pay day," explained Colonel Willey, desperately feigning patience and understanding. "It takes them all day to hand out the pay and get resupplied." The regiment from the 21st division was supposed to have started moving at seven in the morning, but it was already two in the afternoon. "They always have their excuses," said Willey. "No, they're not as motivated as we would like them to be."

There was always the feeling back then, in just the second month of the North Vietnamese offensive, that, of course, sooner or later the South Vietnamese would break through to relieve An Loc—not just by air, as finally happened at the end of June, but by road. "They don't push, they figure it'll eventually get done so why take chances," rationalized Colonel Willey, who'd done a previous combat tour in Vietnam with the special forces. "It's pretty much a Vietnamese syndrome." Then there were always those tantalizingly encouraging intelligence estimates. "We hear rumors the enemy command structure is falling apart," Willey reported, but he himself didn't seem to buy such easy talk. "We still haven't got word that any of the enemy soldiers have begun moving out. We assume parts of three enemy divisions are still in the area around An Loc. . . . We also have rumors that an enemy battalion is cutting the road between our regiments."

Colonel Willey was a rarity in the Vietnam war, an American adviser who wasn't afraid to level with reporters, who refused to accept the corporate optimism of the top command, who deserved and won respect. I saw him almost every day for a while. Then one day in June I got tired of covering the static, stagnating battle for Route Thirteen. That day, back in Saigon, I heard that Colonel Willey had finally been killed by an enemy rocket as he reconnoitered up the road in his jeep. He died near the skeletal watchtower north of Chon Thanh at just the spot where the forward line of South Vietnamese troops were hopelessly dug in, entrenched and immobile, against the North Vietnamese only a few hundred meters away. Nobody knows for sure how many thousands have died for Route Thirteen: perhaps 6,000 South Vietnamese soldiers and twice as many North Vietnamese, not to mention several thousand civilians trapped in An Loc as Communist gunners pummeled it with thousands of mortar, rocket and artillery rounds daily at the height of the fighting. Colonel Willey was just one of the dead, one whom I'd known only slightly but couldn't help remembering with a twinge. Sadness, fear, panic, simple identification with another American? You can never sort out the senses of loss.

There are other memories, too. Phantom, fragmented mental pictures of refugees arriving at a schoolyard in Chon Thanh after walking all the way from An Loc. At first I thought they were happy, overjoyed at escaping after weeks of living in bunkers and holes in the shadows of shelled-out walls, but then I saw they were weeping and moaning. Some of their clothes were soaked in blood. The Communists had fired half a dozen mortar rounds into the group as they trudged down the road midway between An Loc and Chon Thanh. The uninjured had carried the victims to the first South Vietnamese outpost at Chon Thanh. "We had just passed the stream when they began firing at us," said a gray-haired man holding the almost lifeless form of his five-year-old son. "The North Vietnamese did not stop shooting until the airplanes flew overhead. Then we began running away." A little girl and a middle-aged man scrambled from the back of one vehicle with a gap-toothed old lady in their arms. "She is my mother," explained the man, weeping as profusely as his daughter, who was five or six. "She was shot in three places."

And then there was the last American killed in the war. His name was William Nolde, a lieutenant colonel. He didn't begin to participate in the fighting until it was almost over. The many different "fronts" had stabilized, the South Vietnamese had given up the struggle for the road, and the North Vietnamese had almost ceased the shelling of An Loc when Nolde was assigned as senior adviser of Binh Long Province, of which An Loc is the capital. Since the North Vietnamese held the entire province except for An Loc and Chon Thanh, Nolde could do little more than concern himself with advising some of the regional forces on perimeter defense and worrying about the refugees jammed into camps in the next province south. "It's eased off an awful lot," said Nolde, a tall man with a sensitive, slightly swarthy face, when I met him at the end of November. "The big problem is, there's so much lost. The civilians want to go back, but what are the terms of the cease-fire? That's a big question mark." Nolde lived long enough to read the fine type of the Paris agreement as published in *Stars and Stripes* but was killed by a Communist shell that struck his bunker in An Loc on the evening of January 26th, eleven hours before the cease-fire began.

The faces and memories flash before you like random, disjointed shots in a movie, and you hear the long whistle of the bomb and lie waiting for life or death. And it crashes across the road, and you are alive, and you can't understand how it could explode so close and not blast your body into strips of ugly red flesh to rot under the Sunday sun or send the little single sliver of shrapnel through your brain or heart, and you are walking again as the jets gracefully curl away into the blue, and you wonder, can they do this again? They must have expended their bombs by now. But they are a pair—two F-5 Freedom Fighters with six 500-pounders apiece under their chunky sweptback wings—and they are diving one at a time, not together, and they are determined to get you, and they keep returning, dropping one at a time.

We hit it again and get up, and this one has fallen particularly close, just across the narrow blacktop. Engulfed in black billowing smoke, we are choking, unable to breathe for a second, then swallowing and inhaling the smoke, and we know if the next one hits in just the same place it has to get us, and we run through the smoke and into the open daylight as one of the F-5s again rolls in, and we hit it again. Then we hear the crackle of the North Vietnamese AK-47 rifles behind us, and the edge of relief hovers—almost invisible, but still there, over the fear. In four years of covering this war, it is the first and only time I have heard the staccato of the AKs and been glad. The planes now know the North Vietnamese positions and maybe will attack them and not us.

The next time the bomb falls it is at least 200 feet behind us, and we hear the sound of miniguns cutting across the road. I wave my hands as I walk because the pilot now has another target and I want to convince him I am unarmed. The planes have unloaded all their bombs, and they are coming in only for strafing. We keep flinching at the sound of the diving jets, but we are no longer hitting the dirt— miniguns are much more personal, they will kill you just as well lying down as standing. Each time the planes dive the crackle of the miniguns is somewhat weaker. They are apparently strafing the brush on either side far behind us. We keep walking, without jumping now at the screams of the diving jets, and then we see the dots of South Vietnamese soldiers down the road and a tower over the last South Vietnamese outposts, and the fear begins to lift.

We are safe when we cross the first strip of barbed wire across the road, but I raise my feet unnecessarily high over a single strand linked to a mine. Half a dozen South Vietnamese soldiers watch as we stumble back to our car, lungs clogged with bomb smoke, half-breathing, and flop into the seats. One of them offers a drink from his canteen, and we swig and spit out, but we are too tired to shake hands or even say thank you. And we suspect, besides, that some South Vietnamese commander deliberately called in the strikes on top of us to keep reporters from meeting the North Vietnamese, particularly since the window of our car displays a sign saying "bao chi" for reporter. The South Vietnamese, since the cease-fire began, have been battling correspondents constantly to keep them from visiting Viet Cong villages or talking with Communist members of the Joint Military Commission, set up by the agreement. Policemen arrest reporters entering VC "liberated zones" and demand special passes, often impossible to obtain, at the gates of compounds occupied by JMC members. It is probably a bureaucratic error that soldiers at the last outpost on Route Thirteen were not ordered to stop us. Possibly no one in Saigon believed that anyone would venture across a no-man's land still littered with the debris of months of fighting: rusted hulks of rocketed trucks, shell casings, helmets.

If the South Vietnamese are not brave enough to fight for the road on the ground, however, they are glad to have any excuse for bombing at will—in violation of the agreement. They can always say we were caught in a crossfire and cite our case as a warning to other correspondents venturing into "insecure areas." In fact, our survival demonstrates what many analysts of the war have known for years, that airpower alone is hardly an effective weapon. It might be appropriate to end this story as we peer back, John Wayne-style, pursing our brows and scanning the road to see the North Vietnamese banner still flying above the road on the horizon. But we do not look back, we do not ask questions. We just drive and do not talk to each other until reaching a soft drink stand fifteen miles to the south. We get out and gulp down our colas, swallowing hard over the dust in our throats, and my driver notices his watch is gone—lost in one of those dives in the dirt. "You buy me new watch," he says with a grin, and we are alive and laugh. The fighting for Route Thirteen may sputter on for years, but for us the battle is over.

chapter 10:

"Back in the world"

There was still a war to fight "back in the world." For the first time in American history the returning GIs were not greeted as combat heroes. Nor did they particularly *feel* like heroes as they formed pressure groups such as Vietnam Veterans Against the War, staged demonstrations, and demanded better breaks from Congress and the Veterans Administration, attuned to veterans from a different era, with different attitudes. The mood of the GIs, it seemed, reflected not only their experience in Vietnam but also the outlook of an entire society fed up with overseas adventurism.

Like the GIs after their year at war, I returned to the States in late 1971 with a sense of chagrin over the response of Americans to the Vietnam experience. For me, in fact, the sense may have been deeper than it was for most GIs since I had not been home in more than four years, most of that time in Vietnam. It was not the opposition to the war that bothered you, it was the apathy, the misunderstanding of the nature of the war, the lack of concern. "Did you see anyone get killed in Vietnam?" trilled a young society matron in Chicago during a small interlude in a cocktail-party conversation before turning to other more interesting topics. "Did you hear bullets?" asked a Chicago police reporter, apparently influenced by World War II movies. Beneath that level, you discovered, there was not much real interest in what had happened to us in Vietnam.

And yet you had only to talk to Vietnam veterans to confirm that the war had indeed had a deep impact on them and, in some indefinable way, on our entire society as well. I interviewed veterans in New York, Washington, Philadelphia and Chicago, and a number of points in between, and found a common thread of depression and bitterness. It was, perhaps, the best time in the war to conduct such interviews. We were still fighting in Vietnam, but we knew by then the hopelessness of the cause, and the veterans were at a high point of both organized and individual discontent. Somehow it seemed a fitting way to conclude my own impressions of the war, though I was back in Vietnam by the end of the year and wound up covering some of the major battles of 1972. Later, as they merged into the rest of our society, the veterans began to lose some of the edge of their anger. "You can't get anyone organized any more," complained a former army captain, wounded twice in Vietnam, whom I met in late 1973. "The movement has lost its force."

The question remained, however, in what way the veterans, sinking again into the mainstream of American life, would affect those around them, turning their experience in Vietnam into a personal legacy for all of us to bear.

Chicago: October, 1971

Chicken Unlimited sells four- to twelve-bit dinners at

prices ranging from $1.49 to $4.75 at its gaudy white-tiled outlet on South State Street and Garfield Boulevard, but the biggest operator around the corner may be an afro-haired hustler with a deceptively engaging manner and the soul name of Brother Rap, the same soubriquet, as it happened, of another "brother" whom I had met several months earlier on "Soul Alley" in Saigon. "You just need somethin'," says Brother Rap, letting the words slide between almost pursed lips in a low undertone, "you see me." As long as he's convinced you're not a cop or an informer, you can "score skag" with him for "a nickel or dime"—five or ten dollars or even a bargain-basement three dollars for a small capsule. "Good enough to keep you goin' for a little while, anyway."

Brother Rap swears he can answer a junkie's needs "for not too much," but he admits he'll never hustle skag for the low-low rates he used to charge at the army's big logistics post at Long Binh, fifteen miles northeast of Saigon. "I got so used to hustlin' in 'Nam, I kind of dug it," says Brother Rap, talking in the relative sanctuary of the lobby of the Veterans Administration Assistance Center on West Taylor Street. "We got it for a couple dollars a vial and sold it for five. It was ninety-five percent pure around there. Here we have to cut it way down." Brother Rap, who refuses to give his real name for obvious reasons, says he was "puttin' skag myself" for a little while, but he claims he's off it now. "Oh, I snort maybe once or twice a week," he says. "I was shootin' over in 'Nam."

Brother Rap smiles laconically at the memory of injecting heroin into his arm. "I Jonesed on the plane coming back," he says. "Throwin' up and aching all over. The Jones is somethin' else." He shudders at the memory of a typical physical response to coming off heroin. Brother Rap now wants a job—in fact, he's visiting the VA Assistance Center for advice on finding one—but he's not at all certain he can adapt to humdrum routine and regular hours. "I haven't been working for ten months, ever since I got out of the army," he says. "I didn't even want to work. I was a little screwed up. I think I still am." Brother Rap's plight is typical of that of untold thousands of veterans, white and black, who got hooked in Vietnam. "It's impossible to tell the exact effects of the war on the drug problem," says Dr. Edward Senay, director of the Illinois Drug Abuse Program, "but I would estimate that 1,000 of 30,000 addicts in Cook County are Vietnam veterans."

The depth of the drug problem, exacerbated by the wide-open availability of heroin outside literally all U.S. military installations in Vietnam, defies precise analysis in part because most of the victims are not seeking assistance in organized drug programs. "There's so many junkies around here. They all got the habit in Vietnam," says Brother Rap. "They might kick it for a while but then start all over again. Drug programs don't do no good. Man goes there for an overdose. He straightens out for a while. Then he's shootin' up again."

Psychologists and doctors might accuse Rap of some exaggeration, but basically they agree with his view of the difficulties, particularly as reflected among Vietnam veterans. "There tends to be a lag period between the time a person gets strung out initially and the time he comes for treatment," says Dr. John Chappel, clinical psychiatrist with the Illinois Drug Abuse Program, explaining why relatively few Vietnam veterans have approached the program for treatment even though they are given priority above others. "Initially, the individual feels, 'Well, I can kick it myself.'"

Another complication, cited by Dr. Bernard Rappaport, chief of psychiatry at the West Side Veterans Administration Hospital, is the sense of disillusionment shared by most Vietnam veterans, particularly those on drugs. "They don't want to talk about Vietnam," says Dr. Rappaport, who has organized the hospital's drug clinic, the only one operated by the VA in Illinois. "It's difficult for them to discuss their experiences." The result was that almost no Vietnam veterans requested treatment at the clinic, which was capable of caring for thirty bedridden patients and another 200 on an out-patient basis when it opened in August of 1971. "Most of our patients are hard-core addicts, people who've been on drugs for ten or fifteen years," says Dr. Rappaport. "The Vietnam people are just beginning to come as word of our program spreads."

In a small conference room off the drug ward, a one-time marine lance corporal, wounded by shrapnel at Khe Sanh in 1968, tells why he happened to get into the program. "I was shootin' all day before getting into the service," says the ex-marine, in the presence of a couple of young rehabilitation coordinators who forbade him to give his name. "I stopped in basic training, but then I went back in Vietnam. I was high when I went on my first operation." In tones mingling braggadocio with guilt, the ex-marine recounts his success in "ripping off" military post exchanges, in both Vietnam and the States, and then in looting stores and homes in Chicago after his discharge. "It was costing me $150 a day to keep up the habit," he explains. "I was mixing heroin with cocaine and shooting it."

In fact, he says, he might not have abandoned this life of petty crime had he not been sent to the VA hospital for treatment for serum hepatitis, spread by shooting with unsterilized hypodermic needles. "We get all the referrals for hepatitis," interjects one of the rehabilitation coordinators, Joel Laskin, who is studying for his Ph.D. in clinical psychology at Loyola. "We informed him we had a program and asked if he was interested. He was. He's been in the clinic for two months now." The ex-marine, in a real sense, is among the fortunate few, fortunate to have had to go to the hospital with hepatitis before he was finally arrested or hurt in a hold-up, fortunate to have been at a hospital with a new drug clinic, fortunate to have encountered doctors and rehabilitation coordinators personally interested in helping him. His case, as far as I could determine from interviews with a number of veterans, is a rare exception.

"We admit the drug problem caught us by surprise," says a VA official in Washington, noting that the first VA drug clinic was not opened until late 1970. "We're still geared to alcoholics from World War II and Korea," the official goes on. "We already have forty-one alcohol treatment centers and only thirty-two for drugs. We're planning twenty-eight more drug centers and twenty-one new alcohol treatment centers." The VA was so far behind on the drug problem, according to some psychiatrists, that certain of its top administrators opposed extensive treatment for drug addiction. "They're still reluctant to develop an out-patient program," says a Chicago drug expert who requested anonymity. "That's ridiculous since the majority of cases don't require bed care."

As to Brother Rap talking about the sale of drugs on South State Street, he may subconsciously reflect another legacy of Vietnam: its effect upon the attitudes of black GIs after they return to the States. While drug problems cut across racial lines, blacks seem to suffer more and to share a deeper sense of resentment than do white GIs over the effects of the war on their total lives. Whatever their response may have been in individual predicaments in the field, black veterans say the war has united them against whites, has taught them how to fight whites, has steeled their determination to defeat the white majority in some climactic, if vaguely defined, revolutionary conflagration.

"The military did one thing for me," says a sinewy freshman at Chicago's Malcolm X College, toying with a black power bracelet made of shoelaces from his old army boots. "It showed me how screwed up this country really is. Here, people are indoctrinated to the policies of the U.S. In Vietnam you know reality—death. The war made me understand how the system is run, why the white men make wars, what it's like to be in wars. I regret having gone to

Vietnam for fighting," he concludes, biting off his words, "but it showed me the true way of life. I now want to work for the black veterans movement, so we can better ourselves against the white man."

If black and white veterans sometimes seem to share a similar sense of guilt and futility, they differ sharply in both the degree and direction of their anger. Not surprisingly, the former tend to express their resentment against all of white society while the latter focus on the men responsible for sending them to Vietnam, or, at most, on government bureaucracy in general. "Vietnam was a racist war," says Brother Maurice, another Malcolm X student, a machine-gunner with the 25th division who was court-martialed, but not convicted, in Vietnam for refusing to go to the field on one occasion. He was finally discharged as "undesirable" after returning to the States. "They called us 'nigger' and gave us the worst jobs. The black dudes looked after each other's backs in the field. We was pretty heavy with each other."

Brother Maurice's charge of racial discrimination in the army may not be entirely accurate, but there is no doubt the Vietnam experience has added both cohesion and strength to black movements in America. Black GIs generally shared quarters with each other, hung together in the field, formed Black Panther and other organizations at bases, and, at some installations in rear areas, fomented riots against white authority. One obvious symbol of black unity in Vietnam is the DAP, the elaborate handshake ritual by which black GIs greet each other. Now the DAP (the initials are for "Dignity for Afro Peoples") is spreading to the States as black veterans teach their younger soul brothers how to do it.

"The black GIs were like one happy family," says Brother Maurice. "We called the handshake 'the blessing.'" Brother Maurice insists that veterans at Malcolm X do not force students who haven't served in the army to learn the DAP, but the fad is spreading quickly around the school, as proven by the sight of students engaging in the ritual between classes in the cafeteria and in the halls. The search for racial identity among black veterans extends from the symbol of the DAP to the reality of black commando groups, made up of men who were trained by the army to kill and sensitized by the Vietnam experience to hate "white oppressors." A factor in the rage of black commandos, some of them Black Panthers, but many affiliated with underground, unpublicized organizations, is the inability to find jobs in a period of economic recession.

"We have some of the world's best commandos right here in the ghetto," observes Samuel Campbell, a twenty-three-year-old former army sergeant who served in both Vietnam and Thailand and now works full-time for the Committee of Concerned Veterans, an organization formed here to help black GIs find jobs. "These men might not all have salable skills," says Campbell, "but they're expert at firing weapons." And what's more, he says, some of them are hoarding weapons for the time when they can use them. "They may have no other choice." The threat may appear exaggerated, but Campbell points out that hundreds, if not thousands, of blacks in the ghetto received less than honorable discharges as a result of perpetual conflicts with military authorities in Vietnam. They are not only ineligible for Veterans Administration benefits, including hospitalization and education allowances and job advice, but they are also persona non grata at virtually all employment offices.

"They can always say they have honorable discharges," says Campbell, "but sometimes employers will check. Anyway, there aren't many jobs available." As a case in point, he notes that his office once had a request for a dozen housemen to work at a convention and received thirty-six applications within a few hours after spreading the word. Inside the office of the Committee of Concerned Veterans, on the far South Side, several blacks with undesirable or bad conduct discharges talk about their problems. "An undesirable stigmatizes you for life," says a man who was recently laid off from a job on a garbage truck. "You're enslaved. You can't do anything or get anywhere. A man getting out of prison has a better chance of getting a job."

One of the Vietnam veterans boasts that he sent a letter to President Nixon threatening to "blow up the White House with you inside." He shows the calling card of a secret service agent who knocked on his door one day to ask what he meant and to advise him of the illegality of such threats against the President of the United States. "I told him I didn't care what he said, I didn't have a job and I *would* blow up the White House if that's what I had to do to survive," says the black, angrily pounding a tabletop, glaring at me, his interviewer. "I have a family. I have to eat. I'll do anything." The desperation of some of the ghetto-dwellers, including war veterans, often discourages them from participating in essentially white antiwar protests staged by such groups as the Vietnam Veterans Against the War, a nationwide organization. "Our people don't care about the war one way or another," says Campbell. "It's not our war. It takes money to march around in peace groups. We haven't got the time. Why march for peace in Vietnam when you haven't got peace here?"

The blacks, however, are not alone in their distaste for demonstrations and such. A block west of the modernesque towers and walkways of the University of Illinois at Chicago Circle, a rundown shack reverberates with the sound of stereo music mingled with occasional shouts and laughter. The paint on the walls and roof of the shack is chipped and peeling, and the only external visual sign of life inside is a crudely written placard advising visitors to enter by the rear door. The occupants of the shack once adorned it with a banner saying "Veterans' Club," but they had to tear it down after long-time residents of the old Italian neighborhood charged that regulations forbade such "commercial advertising," as if the veterans and the war represented nothing more than an aesthetically displeasing business venture.

"We just set it up as a place where a guy can come here, relax, and try to get away from the sterile atmosphere of the campus," says James R. Janicki, who served a year at the army's logistics center at Long Binh and now is studying for a degree in business administration. "Guys sit around and tell war stories, but we don't talk about gruesome experiences. It's kind of a mixed-up thing." The small talk at the clubhouse, in fact, illustrates the problems and attitudes, the revolt and confusion, among today's veterans, anxious to forget but unable to rid themselves of the memory of their year at war. Open to all 1,200 veterans on the Circle campus, the club, almost entirely white, is typical of hundreds of veterans' social groups at colleges and universities throughout the country. "If anybody comes in here and boasts about how many men he's killed, there's usually a very bad response," says Charles Buccholz, an ex-marine who once went on special reconnaissance missions in the northern provinces of South Vietnam and sometimes strayed across the borders into enemy strongholds in southern Laos and North Vietnam. Buccholz, sitting on a stool in front of the long wooden bar in the dimly lit clubroom, denounces the war as "a waste," but admits he can't stop talking about it—not the encounters with an omnipresent enemy but "the girls you met, the camps you've seen, the old sergeants, leave in Bangkok, stuff like that."

The fact that Buccholz, like most other members of the club, not only opposes the war but refuses to boast about his own exploits indicates the mood of Vietnam veterans, who scorn and often loathe the "old men" from World War II and Korea. "The guys in the Veterans of Foreign Wars and the American Legion look at the war from a different point of view," says Wayne Olenick. "They fought their wars to win, but there's no way we're going to win this war," adds Olenick, a lieutenant with the military police in Saigon during the 1968 Tet offensive, in which thirty-seven MPs were killed. If the members of the Veterans' Club do not identify with their counterparts in the old, established veterans' organizations, however, they still identify with each other and their own war, a phenomenon of possibly far-reaching consequences if the United States ever enters another armed conflict. Not surprisingly, the veterans almost instinctively cling to some of the customs formed in Vietnam. The decor of the club, for instance, resembles that of officers' or NCO clubs at small installations throughout Vietnam. The cheap soft lighting, the beer signs, and the American flag behind the bar all contribute to the effect.

Nor are the veterans antimilitary as such. "I still can't really knock the marine corps," says Buccholz, who left the service as a sergeant and hopes to go to law school. "I just don't believe the marines should have been sent to do something really wasteful." To which Olenick adds: "I would still fight for my country if I thought it was right. I'd probably fight even if it wasn't right." Olenick's "my-country-right-or-wrong" attitude may not jibe with the view of all club members, but few if any are prepared to demonstrate *against* their country, either. "I have no desire to protest," says another ex-marine, Thomas Flaws, who considers the United States the aggressor in Vietnam. "If you have a protest," he says, "it gets out of hand and destroys property." Basically, the members of the Veterans' Club, representative of the majority of students who have served in Vietnam, prefer to remain as noncommitted as possible on social issues, a position that may in itself, in the view of some of their critics, belie passive support of the establishment.

Symbolic of their conventional approach is that some of them would like to introduce Greek fraternity-style letters and perhaps even wear special jackets, social, seemingly nonpolitical gestures that still have deep political overtones if one views the entire fraternity system as basically conservative. "We have people representing all views," says Janicki, one of the club's founders, but the real protesters gravitate toward the Vietnam Veterans Against the War. "Probably eighty percent of the Vietnam veterans don't want to join any kind of protest," says Al Hubbard, executive secretary of the VVAW's executive committee in New York. "They just want to forget about the war and go back to whatever they were doing. They figure they spent two or three years in one organization, the military, and they don't want to join another." The experience of the VVAW at the Circle campus bears out this thesis. The VVAW campus leader, Phil Rubin, who served as an infantryman northwest of Saigon, admits that only a handful of veterans have signified any real interest in joining the campus chapter.

Rubin, who studied engineering at the University of Michigan for two years before he was drafted and now majors in philosophy, wants to do more than catch up. He wants to crusade for complete withdrawal of all American troops from Vietnam. His most persistent enemy is not any serious opposition to his viewpoint but rather the apathy of the students, who, like many other Americans, may not care if the United States maintains a presence in Indochina so long as the war is winding down. Rubin, who has grown his hair in a ponytail since his discharge from the army two years ago, does not look with disdain or dislike on his less radical colleagues. Indeed, he is more likely to view with some contempt the noisy antiwar protests of students who have never served in Vietnam. "Maybe it's an age thing," he says. "I'm twenty-four, three years older than the average kids in my class. Some of the younger ones seem so impetuous. They spout these socialist ideas, and that's great. Then they come up and tell us about Vietnam. I resent that. You can read all the books in the world, and it's not like being there."

As a matter of fact, Rubin may identify more easily with the drinkers at the Veterans' Club than with the protesters on campus. "It's common experience," he says. "You just relate to each other. You see a guy wearing a military patch you recognize, or just walking around in fatigue jacket and boots. Or maybe you hear a word common to GIs in Vietnam, like 'beaucoup' or 'number one' or 'di di' for 'go away.' Other students think we're all nuts. They're convinced we're nuts. All they have to do is sit around and listen to this language thing. They don't understand you." All of which may go to symbolize the alienation of the Vietnam veteran from his environment, in this case the academic community.

There always is, however, a form of rebuttal for those who regard college students, like blacks and drug addicts, as societal rejects or, at best, rebels. Beyond the urban ghetto or the urban campus, there remains the vast expanse of middle-America, home of the fabled silent majority. So I drive some twenty miles south of Chicago to a typical middle-class suburb named Midlothian, a name that somehow catches my imagination as even more mid-American than, say, Highland Park or Wilmette. The American flag flies twenty-four hours a day over Midlothian, whose elders, appropriately enough, have chosen to call it "the community of the lighted flag." The operator of the village's foremost hamburger stand was the first, as noted on a bronze plaque beside the food counter, "to call the nation's attention to the fact that the American flag, when illuminated, can be displayed at night." As a result of the "great public interest in flying the American flag by night," the plaque goes on, "the White House illuminated their [sic] flag August 21, 1970." It is somewhat ironic, then, in view of this effusion of patriotic spirit, that Midlothian's Vietnam veterans should exude the same acute problems, the same sense of revolt, in readjusting to American society as do students at large universities or blacks in the ghetto.

"When I got home, I was really confused," says Ronald McSheffery, sitting at a smooth-paneled table several feet from the plaque, munching a hamburger. "I didn't know whether to like this place or hate it." Perhaps the most shocked and confused were McSheffery's father, James, a carpenter, and his mother, who had just moved into a neat two-story home from which one could always see the American flag flying over a well-manicured high school several blocks away. "I was just about twenty pounds underweight and looked like I had jaundice," explains Ronald, who was granted a general discharge "under honorable conditions" a year ago after rebelling completely against his commanders in Vietnam. "I'd been shooting heroin over there and began coming off it on the plane coming back. My mother was really scared just looking at me. First thing she did was make sure I got my weight back and got some sleep."

Ronald's parents always viewed him as the rebel of the family since he had dropped out of high school after his junior year, but they stopped criticizing him when his older brother, Andy, twenty-one, the oldest of the eight McSheffery youngsters, dropped out of the navy last June 7th. "I thought the war was a big joke, a waste of time," says Andy, whose commander in Vietnam once tried to have him court-martialed for flashing the V-for-peace sign instead of saluting. "He asked me what the sign meant, and I said, 'Peace—no fightin', like the whole thing's solved.' He said, 'What do you mean, peace?' and I said, 'Peace, man—what are you anyway, a warmonger?' Then he called me in his office and gave me a whole thing about respect." Andy's case was so petty that the military court before which he was to appear refused to hear it, but he ran afoul of another commander in Hawaii after completing his Vietnam tour. "He saw me sitting around with my feet on the desk and said if I didn't watch it, I'd get demoted. I said I didn't want any demotion, I wanted my discharge. So I wrote a letter explaining how I felt about the war and the navy, and the bureau of personnel let me out."

The attitudes of the McSheffery brothers conflict not only with the established values of Midlothian but also with those of their own relatives: their father, a World War II veteran; an uncle, a retired chief petty officer in the navy; and another uncle, who once commanded a post of the Veterans of Foreign Wars. Like most Vietnam veterans, the younger McShefferys would not consider a visit to the local VFW post, whose aging members concede they're concerned about the future of the VFW "after we're all gone." Andy, consenting to accompany me on a visit to the bar at the VFW post, looks embarrassed and self-conscious as a couple of World War II veterans shake hands with him and tell him about their tours in Europe a generation ago. "Here's the most decorated man at the post," says a silver-haired railroad detective, pointing to a swarthy man behind the bar. "He was with the marines in the South Pacific in World War II."

Andy listens politely, then, during a break in the conversation, suggests, "It's time we get going." As we are walking out the door, he mutters unhappily about the men at the VFW bar. "What a waste," he says, "they're not even real." If Ronald and Andy McSheffery typify disillusioned Vietnam veterans in terms of attitude and outlook, they also illustrate the desperate search among ex-GIs for jobs, education, and new roots in a society that seems much more alien to them now than when they left home two or three years ago. "I'll do anything," says Ronald. "Wash dishes, sweep floors—anything. I need work. One time there I was filing ten applications a day. They all said, 'We'll call if we have anything.' I never heard." Since returning home in August, Andy has been trying to find a job in construction. "I can't find nothin', so I've gone to bartender's school for a week," says Andy. "Maybe I'll get somethin' there." Alternatively, he may enroll in a community junior college and live on part-time employment and educational benefits from the Veterans Administration.

A depressing factor in the brothers' search for jobs is that more companies are laying off workers while more veterans return from Vietnam. More than 30,000 veterans are looking for work in the Chicago area and another 40,000 will return to the region in the next few months as the last American combat units withdraw from Vietnam. "We're sponsoring job fairs around the state," says a government employment service man, but Ronald reports that personnel representatives at one fair all informed him there were no openings. "They said they just wanted us to know about them in case the situation changed," says Ronald. "It was a big waste of time." Besides, many veterans are too restless to want to resign themselves to long stints with companies that might resemble nothing so much as the army. Both Ronald and Andy reflect the desire to get away from their home, to wander around the country, before settling down.

The cases of Ronald and Andy seem to fit in with attitudes already noted among ex-GIs by Robert Jay Lifton, research professor of psychiatry at Yale, who has conducted studies among veterans protesting the war. "All veterans are in some kind of profound conflict," says Lifton. "No man had a very clear sense of justification of what he did or why we were in Vietnam. They all feel betrayed by this war. Everybody—even those who think we should have fought harder and bombed Hanoi—feels there was something not quite right about this war." It is partly for this reason that veterans often join clubs (not the VFW or American Legion but their own groups) and tend to hang around with each other. "They can only find with each other that authenticity they seek. They may not seek political goals. It's all a question of psychological needs," Lifton reasons. "I can't see leading a regular life," Ronald McSheffery remarks disconsolately, without suggesting exactly what he'd like in its place. "This town is just dull and boring," echoes Andy. "Everybody watches television at night, and that's it."

Epilogue

Not all the returning veterans were forgotten. The exceptions, the ones who really aroused public interest and sympathy, were the prisoners of war. After the deaths and wounds and hardship suffered by so many thousands of Americans in Vietnam, I was somewhat confused and surprised by the emphasis placed upon a handful of GIs in prison camps in North Vietnam or in Viet Cong jungle redoubts in the South. It was not that they personally did not deserve the deepest sympathy and support. It was just that their suffering was exaggerated out of all proportion to that of the many, many more who had died unknown and unmourned except by their immediate families and friends, or else endured untold miseries in field hospitals. Yet, beneath the level of overt concern for the POWs, there was the question of who, beyond their families, really cared about *their* fate either. For the Nixon administration, the existence of the POWs provided an easy rationalization for remaining in the war until conclusion of an agreement providing for their release. For those who opposed the war, visits to POW camps in North Vietnam resulted in facile antiwar propaganda, none of which gave any hint of the duress under which the POWs had to live.

Finally, the release of the POWs seemed to offer a great wet blanket with which the Nixon administration could save face and hide the defeat and failure inherent in the peace agreement. The last surge of POW publicity was deeply embarrassing, not to mention hypocritical and dishonest. While no efforts were spared to insure the successful transition of the POWs to civilian life, information officers barred reporters from talking to any of them, ostensibly for fear the journalists' questions might upset their psyches. In fact, in the view of many who covered the release of the POWs, the Nixon administration was afraid that interviews might result in adverse publicity and criticism and mar the drummed-up spirit of "victory" surrounding "peace with honor." Another reason, perhaps, was that officials may have been afraid the POWs would report tales of torture—and thus jeopardize subsequent releases, spaced out at intervals over a forty-five-day period beginning February 12th. Certainly many of the POWs, after the final release in Hanoi on March 29th, did not hesitate, this time at the urging of Defense Department officials, to reveal the horrors to which they had been subjected in captivity.

Despite a sense of revulsion over the Nixon-serving, show-business aspect of the releases, however, one could not help but find them deeply moving. I watched two of them, one of GIs and civilians held in the South, the other of pilots in Hanoi. The dusk of early evening was just turning to night when the row of helicopters, each flashing red lights on top, appeared in the distance over Tan Son Nhut air base. The helicopters were bearing twenty-seven prisoners from the shell-pocked airstrip of Loc Ninh, a district town captured by the Viet Cong at the beginning of the May, 1972, offensive. It was the first day of the POW releases, and the Viet Cong had finally let them go after a twelve-hour delay during which they had insisted first on the arrival at Loc Ninh, aboard C-130 cargo planes, of some 150 of their own prisoners released by the South Vietnamese. Finally, as reporters watched from behind a cordon guarded by military policemen, the POWs jumped out of the helicopters, laughing and joking, and walked across the tarmac to the waiting C-9 hospital plane as if they were figures in a movie setting.

There they were, wearing blue and green Viet Cong pajamas with American medical tags on them, waving at the row of journalists and photographers one hundred feet away and then shaking hands with Ambassador Ellsworth Bunker and other officials before boarding the plane for the next lap in their homeward journey, the ride to Clark Air Force Base in the Philippines. It was the final moment of ecstasy after a day of agony and frustration that had seemed at moments to cast doubts on the entire prisoner release program. If the ex-POWs were unhappy about the long wait, however, they did not indicate as much as they strolled toward the white-painted C-9. "They all said it's great to be back," said Bunker, who shook hands with each of them by the stairs leading into the rear of the plane. "And we said in return, 'It's great to have you home, it's a great day for all of us.'" By the time of the release, said the brigadier general who had negotiated for the United States in Loc Ninh, "the feeling of satisfaction erased all the bad memories of the long day of waiting."

The atmosphere of the final prisoner release in Hanoi was, if anything, still more tense, partly because most of the reporters who flew there on the Royal Air Lao charter flight from Vientiane had never previously visited the North Vietnamese capital. Our hosts showed us the rubble of bombed-out factories and apartment buildings on the way to one of the camps, which the camp commander gave us to believe had provided an almost idyllic daily diet of volley ball, movies, reading, and studying, not to mention good food. North Vietnamese guards let us view the POWs, standing beside their bunks or in even rows in front of one of the camp buildings, but they forbade us to ask questions. One of the POWs, however, did not seem to care what his captors thought of his remarks as we questioned him through the door of his five-man cell. "It was bad," said Major William James Elander, wearing prison regulation two-toned maroon T-shirt and shorts. "I'll talk about it." It was so bad that Elander was more than a little annoyed with reporters and photographers for seeming to accept just the picture the prison guards wanted to give them of life in the Hanoi Hilton. "We object to these pictures because this is not the way it really is here," said the major, a veteran of two combat tours in Southeast Asia.

"No talk, no talk," the North Vietnamese guards kept telling us as we looked through the bars toward the prisoners standing beside their cots. "Please, it is enough time for you," a guard finally informed me before shutting the windows on several cells of prisoners. A few hours later, on the tarmac of Gia Lam airport, the prisoners stood in even rows, two abreast, unsmiling, as a North Vietnamese officer barked out their names, one by one, in a slightly guttural accent. "American prisoners, listen to your name called and step out," the officer ordered as Air Force Brigadier General Russell G. Ogan waited to welcome each one of them to the American side and point them toward the waiting C-141 Starlifter for the flight to Clark. "Marian, Anthony Marshall," the North Vietnamese officer rasped into the loudspeaker, and Captain Anthony Marshall Marian, first of the last group, walked briskly forward to freedom. Some of the prisoners swallowed slightly as they waited, but none showed any real emotion until saluting General Ogan. Finally, only one of them, Navy Lieutenant Commander Alfred Howard Agnew, was waiting, the last man in the last of four columns. North Vietnamese photographers and soldiers surged around him, forming a circle, smiling and shouting at each other to take pictures.

A North Vietnamese captain, in pith helmet and baggy fatigues, stood beside Agnew, grinning broadly. The young pilot, the last American captured in North Vietnam during the final phase of the bombing in December, grinned, swallowed, and grinned again as his name was called. Then he walked through what now was a gauntlet of North Vietnamese and American reporters and photographers and saluted General Ogan, standing beneath a green parachute under slightly overcast skies. "I'm real glad to see you," he said. "You must be a dignitary with all that delay," the general replied. The crowd of North Vietnamese, several thousand of them in front of the partially destroyed terminal building, broke through security guards and milled across the runway. Agnew, now accompanied by American liaison officers, walked to the plane. "Let's hit it," he said as he reached the gaping rear entrance to the Starlifter, and one of the air force officers sent to Hanoi to expedite the release let out a short yell.

The war—for the Americans—was over. The next stage of the conflict—the struggle between Vietnamese and Vietnamese, all suitably equipped with weapons supplied by their respective benefactors—was about to begin. The outcome, as the GIs had always known, was predictable. Yet the pilots, who never saw the damage they were doing as they swung gracefully down on their targets, were equally ignorant in their view of the future. "We negotiated a satisfactory conclusion," one of them remarked later, in a talk before a group of wide-eyed schoolchildren. "I am confident we achieved our aims. That's why we fought, and that's why I am here."

As the marine remarked at Khe Sanh, "Tell it to the dead."

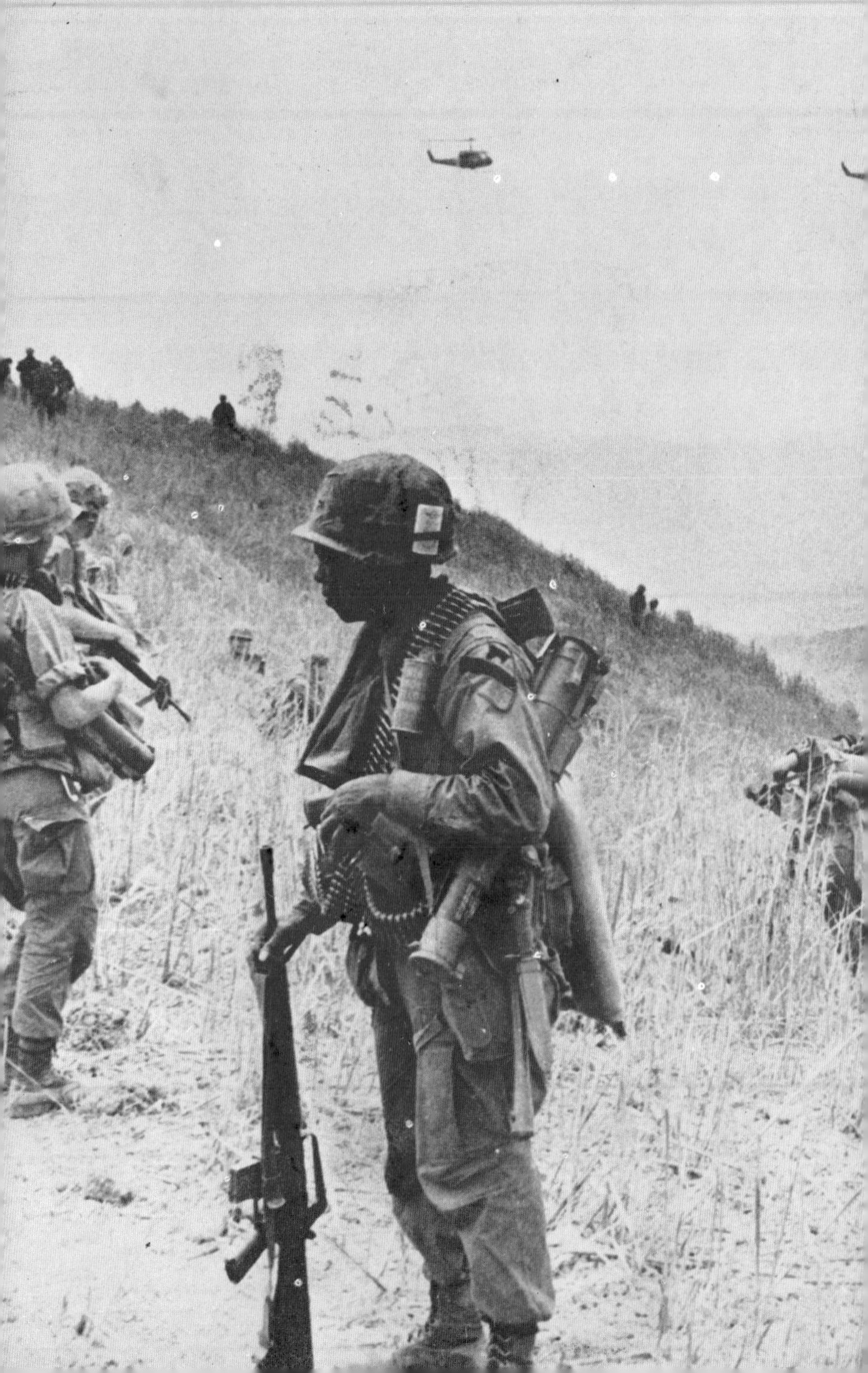